FROM GREENHORN TO SENIOR BOY

My Secondary School Days

FROM GREENHORN TO SENIOR BOY

My Secondary School Days

Robert Peprah-Gyamfi

Perseverance Books

FROM GREENHORN TO SENIOR BOY
My Secondary School Days

Published by Perseverance Books

For information please contact:
Perseverance Books, P.O.Box 8505, Loughborough, LE11 9BZ, UK

www.peprah-gyamfi.com

ISBN: 978-0-9570780-8-6

Table of Contents

Foreword

I think there are two categories of readers who will find this book a very interesting and absorbing read – those looking back, and those looking forward; like the Greek god Janus with two faces – the one looking back and the other looking forward! This may not be the author's intention, since he is really writing for the young person looking forward – who faces the perhaps daunting prospect of overcoming the hurdles and challenges of secondary school life, especially the challenges that face the boarding school boy or girl about to leave home to adjust to a new set of friends and circumstances in a new environment. What young person about to start a new term at a new school does not do so without a sense of apprehension – what will the new academic subjects be like, the new teachers and will there be any pranks played on him or her by the senior students? Foremostly, will he or she succeed in passing the exams? For the young readers in this category the book will be invaluable, for it will provide unlimited encouragement by a writer who himself overcame apparent insurmountable difficulties in his educational career. For them he has a message that one should 'never, never, never give up' – to use Churchill's words to young people in an address he gave at a school during the Second World War. The book is written with humour and sympathetic insight and will give young readers all the encouragement and reassurance they need to know that it is worth putting their hands to the plough and not looking back.

Those who can look back with impunity and pleasure are those, like me, who belong to the second category of readers – those who will find in this book echoes of the trials, tribulations and joys of their own schooldays. In fact, readers in this category may be widespread, not just mature readers who went to school in Africa, but anywhere else in the developing and developed worlds. Mature readers like me who were also educated under the ex-British colonial system in Africa, will find many memories stirred, memories to make them laugh and even, perhaps, shed a tear of remorse; and I venture to say that readers in England and even in the New World will find many common memories, for the English educational system was widespread and, besides, human nature is the same wherever we were brought up. When you come to think of it, the old British system of secondary school education is part and parcel of the education meted out to what is known as the 'baby boomers' – those of us who were born during and just after the Second World War, and we are now living all over the world. Like me, many of these readers will relate to the tribulations of 'homeing' or initiation ceremonies and traditions when they joined a new school or even a new university. I myself was subjected to the most impossible tasks in my first year of residence in university. I was called a 'sprog', had to call the senior students 'sir' and was woken up in the middle of the night to light their cigars. And then which one of us did not sit up late through the night to undertake mental 'mining' expeditions the night before an exam? There is a whole range of memories like these that will be evoked in this book. And for the reader in the West, the differences between his or her own experiences and those of the young boy in Ghana will be fascinating. While the culture might have been different, the human nature is always the same. I personally read this book with a great deal of pleasure and, indeed, a great deal of nostalgia.

Charles Muller
MA (Wales), PhD (London), DEd (SA), DLitt (UOFS).

Acknowledgements

M y thanks go to God Almighty, for the imparting of wisdom needed to write this book.

Rita, my wife, together with our children Karen, David and Jonathan, also deserve my thanks and appreciation for their support and encouragement to successfully conclude this work.

I am also grateful to Dr Charles Muller of Diadembooks.com for carrying out the editorial work on the manuscript and for writing the foreword.

Finally, I am deeply indebted to Rev Anthony Osei-Dankwa, Oda Secondary School Year Group 77, Senior Pastor, Kingdom Life Ministries (aka KLM), London, UK, for confirming the accuracy of some of the dates and times mentioned in the book.

-1-
Struggling hard to embark on my momentous journey

❖

'Oda! Oda! Oda!' I shouted at the top of my voice as I flagged down a vehicle that was approaching the outskirts of our little settlement, still about 300 metres away from where I stood.

As the vehicle drew closer to me, the waving and shouting on my part increased in intensity.

'Stop, please stop!' I kept shouting.

The vehicle approached me, maintaining a constant speed. The driver seemed to pay no attention to the teenager requesting him to stop. At last, he responded to me – not favourably, though. Turning his face towards me for a moment, he gesticulated with one hand indicating that there was no seat left for me.

With disappointment written all over my face, I could only watch the heavily laden vehicle as it crawled along the rugged road that cut through the middle of our village, dividing it in almost two equal halves.

As the vehicle drove on, it churned up a trail of thick dust. Though it was September, and we were not anywhere close to the dry season, which in our part of the country set in from around the middle of December and lasted till the end of February, for the last several days the rains had stayed away.

The state of the Nkawkaw- Akim Oda road! Ever since I was big enough to understand, there had been talk of plans by the government to put asphalt on the main trunk road linking the two most important towns

1

in the area: Nkawkaw, about 30 kilometres to the north of our village, and Akim Oda, about 70 kilometres to the south of us.

Even as I was surrounded by the thick cloud of dust that momentarily threatened to suffocate me, I recalled that putting asphalt on the road was one of the election promises of the MP for our area during the parliamentary election campaign two years before. Since his party won the election and formed the government of the day, not only had he not shown up in the area, but nothing had been heard about his promise.

Whereas his opponents accused him of a breach of electoral promise, his party faithfully responded by saying it was too early to make the accusation since the party had been in power for less than two years.

It was not then the right time to engage in big political issues, however. On that particular day, as far as I was concerned, what was important for me was to find a vehicle that would convey me safely to Akim Oda, to the premises of the Akim Oda Secondary School to be precise. I had been admitted as a Form One student, and it was the opening day for first year students. The rest of the student population were expected in school the next day.

Though disappointed that I was refused a place in the vehicle, I nevertheless understood the driver's reason for rejecting me – the vehicle was chock-a-block full of passengers, with no seats available. As if that were not enough, three male passengers stood on the tailboard of the vehicle, each of them holding tightly to part of the wooden frame that formed the roof, for support.

As I blew the dust off my neatly ironed school uniform – khaki trousers with a blue short-sleeved shirt – I could only hope that it would not be hours before the next bus turned up, and that when it arrived there would be room for me! Partly as a result of the poor state of the road, and also due to the rural nature of the area of the country we lived in, there was very little by way of vehicular activity along the road.

As the day progressed without me getting the opportunity to embark on my momentous journey, I became quite unsettled. Would I get the opportunity to travel that day at all? Or would I be forced to postpone my journey that day and hope for better luck the next day?

Finally, just after midday, another vehicle appeared on the horizon, heading towards the village. I kept praying for a better outcome. As it approached me, at first it seemed the driver was going to ignore my signal to stop. Indeed, it drove past me! But just as my heart sank with the thought that I had missed the last available lift that day, it unexpectedly pulled to a stop!

The driver's mate, who was standing on the tailboard for lack of space within the vehicle, hurriedly got down, took up a wooded 'choc' and placed it behind one of the two rear tyres. Those not conversant with the mechanisms of the vehicle might wonder why this extra precaution was needed. Didn't the vehicle possess a handbrake that could be applied to keep it stationary? My guess is that the handbrake was probably not functioning properly. Even if it did, it probably would not have prevented the overloaded vehicle from rolling backwards!

'Where are you heading for?' the driver's mate asked.

'Akim Oda,' I replied.

'Well, as you can see for yourself, there are no seats left. Fortunately a few of the passengers will alight at Afosu. You will have to stand between the rows until we get there.'

'Thank you very much for your help!' I shouted on the top of my voice. Though having to stand between the rows for the approximately six- kilometre drive to Afosu was not an optimal solution, everyone present – me, my parents, my sisters and friends who had gathered to bid me farewell – were relieved because at long last, I was able to start my journey.

My two dedicated companions

❖

Accompanying me on my journey were two 'companions', a metal box measuring about 70cm in length, 40cm in width and 20cm in height, and a slightly smaller wooden box. Probably because it hardly allowed any air into its interior once it was shut, the metal box became generally known in Ghana as *airtight.*

In Ghana the 'airtight' was usually painted black; red heart-like figures about five centimetres apart from each other stood out in relief against the predominantly black background and gave this airtight box the typical look that came to be associated with it.

The main disadvantage, as I said, was that it hardly allowed air into it when closed. Thus when left locked for a long period of time, the items in it tended to develop a musty smell. This disadvantage was hardly an issue since the need to open it at regular intervals to remove an item or lock away something arose throughout the day.

My other companion, the wooden box, was also popularly known as the 'chop box'. The *Standard English Dictionary* defines the word 'chop' as 'cut – hew – hack – mince – slash – split'.

In Ghana the word 'chop' has gained an additional connotation – it also refers to the act of eating. Thus a fast food restaurant is generally referred to as a 'chop bar' by residents.

From what I have just explained in regard to the usage of the word 'chop' in Ghana, the reader will deduce what kind of role was assigned to my second companion. Then, as now, each student leaving for boarding school fills his or her chop box with provisions.

One might wonder why, then, there was a need for such a box in a boarding school when, as the name suggests, the school authorities are expected to feed students admitted to their various schools. The reason for this will become clear in the course of my narration.

One might ask what type of provisions the chop box carried. The answer is that it varied, depending on the students' tastes and their parental background.

Regardless of the taste and background of the student, however, some items were regarded as 'never-misses' in each chop box. The first item in this category was *garri*, a ready-to-serve meal prepared from the tuber of the cassava plant. Known also as the student's companion, *garri* is popular not only with students in Ghana but also with the general population of several West African countries.

For the sake of those not conversant with this typical companion of a boarding school student in Ghana, I will provide a short description. The cassava plant, also known elsewhere as *manioc*, is a perennial plant that grows best in tropical, moist, fertile, well-drained soil. A completely grown plant may reach a height of about two to four metres. About eight to ten months after planting, long, globular roots or tubers, each with an average weight of about half a kilogram, sprout from the stem just below the soil surface.

The tubers are cleaned after harvesting, then grated – water and starch being squeezed out of the resultant mash which is then left to ferment; it is then roasted to obtain a fine coarse granular flour of varying texture – *garri.*

Most students in Ghana eat *garri* either 'soaked' in cold water, sugar and milk or with a tin of mackerel or sardines added to the *shito,* a hot specially prepared sauce.

Apart from *garri*, other provisions to be found in the student's chop box were sugar, canned milk, canned fish (sardines, tuna, mackerel, etc.), corned beef, as well as *shito*.

Apart from food items, students also filled the wooden box with toiletry items such as soap, toothbrush, toothpaste, body cream, etc.

-3-
'Oversize' and 'undersize': travellers competing for limited space

◈

A t long last, with the help of a *watonkyene* I was permitted to begin my momentous journey.

The *watonkyenes*! One could write volumes about them. Though they are no longer permitted to be used to carry passengers, in those early days they were a very important source of human transport in Ghana – not only in the countryside but in the large towns and cities.

In large cities such as Accra, they were used as tro-tro to transport commuters within the city. In the countryside, they were used not only to transport passengers, but also to cart from place to place various kinds of goods, especially foodstuffs.

They were trucks of the Bedford make. They possessed two cabins. The front cabin was small and constructed from metal. It offered room for the driver and two passengers. The second cabin could be described as a huge wooden cage. Within it, arranged in rows of about seven, were long wooden seats, like benches, each seat providing space for about five passengers.

It is no secret that human beings vary in size. It happened that some passengers, endowed with large buttocks, claimed double, if not more of the space expected of an average passenger! Still, if only for reasons of economics, the drivers usually insisted that the seats were occupied by the minimum number of passengers earmarked for them. If one happened to occupy the same seat as one or even more oversize passenger(s) one could literally be squeezed to the bare bones, just the way sardines are squeezed into their cans.

-4-

Reflections on my journey to the 'Pride of the Akim Kotoku District'!

❖

As the *watonkyene* taking me to 'college' crawled along the rugged road and headed towards Akim Oda, I reflected on my journey.

The journey I was embarked upon, without doubt, marked a defining moment in my life.

Those not familiar with the prevailing situation in the country at that time might wonder why I should regard a move from the elementary to the secondary school as a turning point in my life. Indeed, elsewhere in the world, especially in the developed world, the admission of a pupil to a secondary school might be described as a normal way of life. That pupil might choose to be a day student or move to the boarding school – nothing extraordinary about that.

The situation was quite different in Ghana at the time in question. Gaining admission into a secondary school, whether as a day or boarding student, was beyond the dreams and expectations of the majority of children. For someone like me, it could indeed be seen as hitting the jackpot!

For the sake of those unfamiliar with the Ghana educational system at the time in question, I would like to pause, for a moment, to give a brief overview. It consisted basically of three cycles. The first-cycle, also known as elementary school, took ten years to complete. The first six years of the elementary school was attended in a primary school. For years 7 to 10 of their elementary education pupils moved into the middle school. The middle school ended with the middle school leaving certificate. Probably alluding to the fact that the examination took place in large halls, it was also generally referred to as 'hall'. Thus in those days it was common to hear people speak of going to sit the 'hall'! A holder of the middle school leaving certificate could find work as a factory hand, clerical assistant, pupil teacher, etc.

After obtaining the middle school leaving certificate, one could proceed to do four years at a teacher training college to qualify as a 'trained teacher'. 'Trained teachers' thus played in a 'higher league' as compared to 'pupil teachers'.

The elementary school pathway of education was the remit of the children of the lower class of society – peasant farmers, factory hands, low income earners, the unemployed, etc.

Then there was the secondary school or second-cycle education system. The first part of this took five years to complete, at the end of which students sat for the general certificate of education, ordinary level (GCE 'O'-Level) examinations.

Those who performed well could proceed to do a two-year sixth-form course at the end of which they sat for the general certificate of education, advanced level (GCE 'A'-Level) examinations.

Three passes at the 'A'-Level could open the way for one to study in one of the three universities existing in the country at that time.

In contrast to the first-cycle schools, which were spread throughout the country, the second-cycle schools (secondary schools) were located mainly in districts and regional capitals as well as the national capital, Accra, itself.

How could children who lived far away from such locations also benefit from secondary school education? As a way out of the problem, most of the secondary schools operated on a boarding school basis.

To gain admission to a secondary school at that time, one had to pass an assessment test – the common entrance examination. This was organised once a year in March by the West African Examinations Council. The examining board is a legacy from colonial times. It was set up by the English colonial administration to cater for the schools in their West African colonies – Sierra Leone, Gambia, the Gold Coast (later Ghana) and Nigeria. The test was written simultaneously by all pupils wishing to enter the second-cycle school in all the named countries. A minimum of six years of first-cycle education was required of candidates wishing to sit for the test.

The children of the affluent middle class were generally referred to in Ghana as *Dadamma* (Dada's children), alluding to the fact that such children called their fathers 'Dada', and were usually sent to special primary schools where they were coached specially to pass the common entrance examination. These schools became known as preparatory schools.

The sons and daughters of ordinary citizens, known in society as *Agyamma* (Agya's children) because they referred to their fathers as 'Agya' instead of 'Dada', on the other hand, attended the public elementary schools. Hardly any child there attempted the common entrance exam before they reached middle form three or form four, corresponding to nine and ten years of elementary school education respectively.

It was one thing passing it; it was another matter whether one's parents could afford the costs of education at that level – though, as mentioned elsewhere, tuition at that time was free, from the elementary school up to university, since many of the secondary schools were boarding schools. However, whereas the rich might have considered the boarding and lodging fees as mere peanuts, to the ordinary citizen the fees amounted to a fortune.

In March 1971, as a Form 3 (Year 9) pupil, I sat the common entrance examination. Out of a total of about 60 candidates from my school who attempted the test, only I and one other candidate were successful.

Though I could have opted for several other schools when completing the common entrance forms, I selected Akim Oda Secondary School, popularly known as Odasco, without much forethought. Indeed at that time Odasco had become part and parcel of our family psyche. Four years prior to my admission, in June 1967 to be precise, Ransford, the second oldest child of my parents had completed his GCE 'O'-Level education there.

Indeed, at that stage in my life, I was not aware of any better school to attend than Odasco, the pride of the Akim Kotoku District!

-5-

The law enforcers impeding our progress

❖

I t took about five hours to travel the distance of barely 70 kilometres from Mpintimpi to Akim Oda! Those unfamiliar with the circumstances on the ground might wonder at the unusually long travel time. For such readers, I shall offer a brief explanation.

In the first place, the Bedford truck, whose age I put at no less than 20 years, could barely manage a few kilometres per hour. Earlier on, I also spoke about the bad state of the road we travelled on. Added to this was the fact that the vehicle was overloaded, not only with passengers but also their accompanying luggage.

Furthermore, the vehicle pulled to a stop at almost every hamlet, village or town along the route to allow passengers to disembark, embark, or both.

As if these reasons for delay were not enough, there were numerous police barriers along the way to hamper our progress! The moment the law enforcing agents manning a post spotted our crawling vehicle in the distance, one of them would position himself or herself in the middle of the road and raise one arm straight towards the heavens. Our driver, however reluctantly, had no option but to bring the vehicle to a halt.

Those of us who, on each such occasion, thought the police would surely officially charge or fine the driver for overloading the vehicle would soon learn something else. No sooner had the vehicle pulled to a halt than the police officer, in a seemingly threatening voice, would instruct the driver to meet him at the rear of the vehicle. Instead of

13

issuing a note to officially charge or fine him, a short exchange of words would usually take place. In the process the driver would be observed quickly reaching for his purse and placing 'something' either directly into the pocket of the officer or into his/her palm.

As soon as the 'law enforcing' officer was assured of the safe receipt of the 'gift', he/she would head for the makeshift wooden barrier, raise it, and give us free passage. As the 'old timer', heavily laden with its weary human cargo, a good majority of them sweating profusely from the effect of the scorching African sun, resumed its tortuous journey, the police officers would heartily wave us goodbye.

The soppey chasers from Oda Nkwanta

❖

After the slow, agonising journey over the dusty and rugged road, we made a stop at yet another small town on the route. The signboard displayed prominently on each side of the road informed us of its name – Oda Nkwanta.

'Oda Nkwanta! We're almost there!' I said to myself. Though not very conversant with the names of all the towns and villages along the route we travelled (I had travelled along the route on only one previous occasion), the name Oda Nkwanta rang a bell in my ears. Ransford had on several occasions mentioned that village when narrating some of his Odasco experiences.

He told us that his boarding school served them not only rich food but also food in abundance – to the extent that usually there was surplus food left after each meal. News of the surplus food at the boarding school soon spread to Oda Nkwanta, the nearest village from the institution, about two kilometres to the north. Every evening, not only boys and girls from the village but also the youth and young adults streamed to the perimeters of the dining hall building and waited for the kitchen staff to hand them their leftovers, a term that was better known as *soppey,* meaning surplus food.

Finally, about ten minutes after leaving Oda Nkwanta, we reached the gates of Odasco.

Though our admission letters had urged us to report to the school early to allow us sufficient time to go through the necessary admission procedures, owing to factors the reader is already familiar with, we pulled to a halt at the gates of the school just before the fall of darkness.

-7-
The village boy's fascination with electricity

❖

M y first impression of Odasco was exhilarating, to put it mildly. The school was established in September 1960 by the Ghana Education Trust, a trust enacted by the government of the newly independent country and charged with the construction of new secondary schools, teacher training colleges and other institutions of higher learning to accelerate the educational development of the newly independent country. It was built from scratch at a location that had previously been farmland.

I was fascinated by the sight of several modern buildings that unfolded before my eyes.

As I mentioned earlier, I arrived just at the fall of darkness. Today, thanks to the national electrification programme begun in the 1990s, Mpintimpi and several parts of rural Ghana have the benefit of electricity. The situation was different at the time I was admitted to Odasco. Taking the Akim Kotoku district as an example, apart from the capital, Akim Oda, hardly any town in the district was supplied with electricity.

One can imagine how thrilled the village boy was – a boy who until then had resorted to Swiss kerosene lamps to find his way in the dark – to behold the bright electric lights that illuminated not only the buildings but also the streets.

Then there were the neatly-mown green lawns, the well-laid asphalt roads that snaked their ways around the school compound to link one place with the other. Along the edges of the meandering roads were

17

well-trimmed hedges made up of a combination of beautiful flowers. I was aware that I was taking a leap forward not only in my academic career, but in matters relating to my standard of living as well.

-8-
The colourful dormitories

✦

During my days at Oda Secondary School the male students were housed in two large building blocks. Each building boasted two storeys. Each storey was referred to as a 'house', and there were four houses in all.

As I learnt on my arrival, in former times the four houses were named after the colours Red, Green, Blue and Yellow. The Red and Green Houses shared the same building block, the Blue and Yellow Houses sharing the other. The two buildings were separated by a distance of about 50 metres.

In the course of time, the authorities decided to rename the houses after prominent personalities of the area and beyond, past and present. Eventually Blue House became Frimpong Manso House; Green House, Danquah House; Red House, Attafuah House; and Yellow House, Ahenkorah House.

At the time of my admission to Odasco, the female students were housed in a single-storey building, which looked exactly like those housing their male counterparts.

As in the case of the male students, there were four female houses, where each half of the floor of a storey formed a 'house'.

Also, as in the case of the male students, in former times the female houses were named: Blue, Yellow, Red and Green Houses; at the time of my admission they had been renamed Asantewaa A, Asantewaa B, Sakum A and Sakum B respectively.

Each female house was affiliated with a male house in the following order:

Asantewaa A – Frimpong Manso;
Asantewaa B – Ahenkora;
Sakum A – Attafuah;
Sakum B – Dankwah.

-9-
The Greenhorn and the impossible commands

❖

Before I continue my narration I shall ask the reader to bear with me as I make a brief digression to explain the term *homoing* as used in second-cycle boarding schools in Ghana.

I cannot say for sure when exactly the practice of *homoing* was introduced in boarding schools in Ghana. Neither can I say for sure from whose idea it originated.

Mfantsipin Secondary School in Cape Coast, established in 1876, was the first secondary school in the country. Initially it was run as a day school. In the course of time, it admitted only full boarders.

Perhaps it was the early boarders of Mfantsipim School who first came up with the practice of *homoing*. My research for this book did not uncover any sources to confirm this. What remains an undisputable fact, however, is that at some stage the practice spread to every second-cycle boarding school in the country, becoming in the end part and parcel of the boarding school experience or tradition.

'What, then, *is homoing*?' someone not familiar with the practice might ask.

I wish I could provide a straightforward definition of the term! Though everyone who has passed through the walls of a second-cycle boarding school in Ghana experienced it in one form or the other, the problem begins when it comes to providing an exact definition of it!

The other day, I chanced upon the blogging site of a lady who was reminiscing about her boarding school experience in Ghana. Just as in my case, she was also in a dilemma as to how exactly to define the term.

Is it harassment, is it torture, is it bullying, or just plain initiation – the practice whereby Form One students entering a boarding school for the first time are subjected to various forms of treatments, mostly unpleasant?

In the military, new recruits are made to undergo a period of intensive drilling with the goal, among others, of instilling discipline into them and getting them to obey orders. Was *homoing* introduced into boarding schools in Ghana to achieve a similar goal?

Here I would like to introduce the reader to a few forms of *homoing* as practised during my boarding school days. I beg those who are already familiar with the practice, indeed, those who might have experienced even more severe forms of *homoing* themselves, to bear with me for a while – for the sake of those not familiar with the practice.

Adanko! Adanko is the Twi word for *rabbit*. In this form of *homoing*, the *greenhorn* is required to cross their arms to hold the ear on the other side of the body, squat and in the squatting position move up and down several times. How long the *greenhorn's* ordeal lasted depended entirely on the discretion of the senior student; usually it lasted several minutes.

On your knees! The *greenhorn* could be asked to kneel down for any fanciful reason! Indeed, the practice of kneeling down was one of the most common forms of *homoing*.

Was the senior student in a bad mood, the cause of which the luckless *greenhorn* had nothing to do with? 'Hey you *greenhorn*, why are you looking at me with an evil eye? Get down on your knees!' the order would be shouted.

Had the senior student possibly fared badly in an exam? He/she could vent his/her frustration on the poor Form One student with a dose of *homoing* that involved kneeling down for a considerable period of time.

A senior student who chose to stay up late into the night, usually to learn for an impending examination and, not wanting to 'keep the watch' alone, might just choose to awake some *greenhorn*s from their deep slumber and ask them to kneel beside his bed to keep him company!

To aggravate the suffering of the *greenhorn*, the senior student could decide initially to spread some *garri* on the floor before asking the junior student to kneel on the rough, bristly, grain-like stuff.

The junior could also be made to carry a fully loaded chop box or airtight whilst kneeling down.

March past! As an individual or in a group, the *greenhorn* could be made to march around for an indefinite period of time. As in the case of *kneeling down,* the *greenhorn* could simultaneously be asked to carry a loaded chop box or airtight.

Impossible commands! The *greenhorn* could be ordered to carry out an order that may well be described as an *impossible command.* For example one senior student could order a *greenhorn* to tell another senior student standing close by to their face that, he/she was a *big fool, an idiot* or a *silly billy!* What should the *greenhorn* do in such a situation? Carry out the instruction and face the retribution of the insulted senior, or disobey the command and face the reprisal of the other fellow?

Though several years have elapsed since my student days, I recall that on such occasions I personally acted in line with the proverb: silence is golden. I did not go scot-free for keeping quiet however – a dose of *homoing* of some kind was invariably meted out to me.

Feed the hungry senior! There were occasions when a senior student, returning to the dormitory from wherever, awoke all first year students from their sleep.

'Why are you sleeping when I'm hungry!' he would yell at the top of his voice. 'Hurry up, get to your various chop boxes and get me something to eat!' Needless to say the poor greenhorns hurried out of their beds and did his bidding.

Pillaring! A greenhorn could also be called upon to engage in 'pillaring', which involved having to stand in the same position for a period of time without moving. One could be made to 'pillar' as long as the senior student wished.

Sometimes one could be asked to *pillar* or kneel or *adanko* beside the bed of a senior who would be lying in his bed – reading, relaxing or preparing to go to sleep for the night. The individual could in the process fall asleep, leaving the poor *greenhorn* still dutifully performing whichever act of *homoing* he had been asked to engage in!

If one dared to face the consequences of doing so, one left the scene after a while. Those afraid of the consequences kept on performing whatever they had been asked to do until either the senior student woke up or another senior student chanced on the scene and relieved the poor *greenhorn* of his ordeal.

Though rare, the practice sometime led to injuries. Though I did not personally experience or witness anything of that nature, rumours occasionally made their rounds at Odasco that spoke of *greenhorns* in other schools who had suffered severe, even in some cases life-threatening, injuries.

Homoing was intense in the first several days of the academic year and reduced in intensity after the first few weeks. Still, a Form One student remained a *greenhorn* throughout the academic year and could at any time be subjected to *homoing* by a senior student for any reason.

Homoing was not restricted to the male dormitories; it was practised in the female dormitories as well.

As one might surmise, the practice of *homing* was not sanctioned by the school authorities. That is not to say that the school authorities were unaware of it. The majority of them were themselves products of the Ghana educational system. Having passed through the walls of various second-cycle boarding schools, they themselves had at one stage been victims and perpetrators.

During the first several weeks at Odasco, I was subjected to all the kinds of *homoing* listed above in various forms and intensities. Indeed, on not a few occasions, I wished I was back home in my little village!

One can therefore imagine the sigh of relief that passed my lips when I headed home for the first term holidays. Though I would remain a *greenhorn* for the rest of the academic year, *homoing*, in the form that I was subjected to on quite a regular basis during the first term, would be a thing of the past.

*   *   *

The question the reader might want to ask me is: having been a victim of *homoing* as a *greenhorn*, did you also become a perpetrator?

It will be far from the truth to categorically deny that I did not subject anyone to the practice. Without doubt, I, on a few occasions as a senior student, also ordered, without any apparent reason, I must admit, a *greenhorn* to 'go down on their knees!'

On other occasions, acting alone or together with some of my friends, I also asked a *greenhorn* or a group of them to donate provisions from their chop boxes, to help fill our not fully filled stomachs before retiring to bed.

I cannot however recall subjecting anyone to an extreme form of the practice, the type that inflicted extreme forms of suffering or distress.

If anyone reading these lines is of the view that my account does not correspond to the truth, indeed the whole truth, that individual is welcome to contradict me!

First lessons in tie tying

❖

Not only was the first week a week of intense *homoing*, it was also a week of induction for Form One students. For some of our peers who had attended preparatory schools as boarders, boarding life was nothing new. For Form Ones like me, it was an entirely new experience. During the first week, students like me were assigned tutors from the more senior classes to help familiarise us with boarding school life. Among other things they were to ensure that students like me acquired the following skills:

Proper use of cutlery: Back home at Mpintimpi, I had been brought up to resort to *my natural set of cutlery* (my hands!) to eat my meals. I wished I could continue the practice at the boarding school! But no; each student was required to eat with the conventional set of cutlery – knife, spoon, fork.

Brushing of teeth : Then there was the issue of how to clean my teeth in my new environment! At boarding school, we were required to use a toothbrush and toothpaste!

At Mpintimpi I resorted to chewing sticks such as *tweapea* and *nsorkodua* to do that. For those not familiar with *tweapea* and *nsorkodua*, I shall provide a short explanation. They belong to the Garcinia species of plants. Such plants are noted for their chemical properties that help to protect tooth decay and remove bad breath. The process of cleaning the teeth with those traditional means involves chewing one end of the stick into a brush or tuft and using it to clean the teeth the way one would use a toothbrush. After a while, the tuft is consumed; one has to chew on the stick some more to replace or renew the tuft. The time one spends cleaning the teeth with a stick varies, and depends on how much time one has at one's disposal.

Tying a Tie: Odasco had a special school tie for male students. (The custom of females putting on a tie was not common practice.) We were expected to put on the school tie for Sunday evening service and also for special occasions such as speech and prize-giving days. It goes without saying that someone like me, at the time, had no idea how to tie a tie!

-11-
Abandoned wheel rims disturb our early morning rest

❖

A typical school day began with the sounding of the wake-up bell at 5:30 a.m. Our wake-up bell reminded me of the call-to-worship bell of the Presbyterian church of Mpintimpi. Like the church bell in the little village, its main component was the metal rim of the wheel of an abandoned vehicle. With the help of a metal chain, the rim was hung on a supporting wooden structure that rose to about a metre above the ground. As in the case of the village bell, it was sounded with the help of a piece of iron rod, about 20 centimetres long.

A *greenhorn* dared not ignore the wake-up bell! A senior student of the dormitory went around with a leather belt in hand to give each *greenhorn* he found still in bed a taste of the whip!

On getting up, we rushed to have our shower. There was a large shower room, one for each building, that boasted about a dozen showers. Not everyone was keen on having a shower at that time of day – some deferred that duty to later in the day when lessons were over; others deferred it for a couple of days.

Whether one preferred a morning shower or not, everyone was expected to be ready for morning assembly. By 6:30 a.m. most of us were heading for the assembly hall, which happened to be situated midway between the female and male dormitory blocks.

The morning assembly began with a short devotion at 6:45 a.m. Though a state school, during our time the meditation was Christian based.

It is worth mentioning here that the population of Ghana at that time was about 60 percent Christian, 20 percent Muslim, with 20 percent belonging to neither faith. The Muslim population was confined mostly to the north of the country, far away from the confines of our school.

The meditation, which lasted about 15 minutes, began with a short prayer followed by the singing of a hymn, a reading of a passage from the Bible, a short word of exhortation, a second hymn and the final prayer.

Before we dispersed to our classrooms, the announcements for the day – if there were any – were read out either by the master on duty, the senior housemaster, the assistant headmaster or the headmaster himself, as the case might be.

From there we headed for our various classrooms. Classes began at 7:15 a.m., with two periods, each lasting 45 minutes after which there was a break for breakfast. Classes resumed at 9:30 a.m. with six more lesson periods interrupted by short breaks of five to ten minutes. Finally at 1:45 p.m. the bell went for the end of lessons. At that point the whole school streamed to the dining hall for lunch.

Lunch was followed by siesta lasting an hour. In theory every student was expected to spend the time resting in his or her bed. In practice, however, only students in the junior classes, mainly Forms One and Two, adhered to the rule, albeit not voluntarily – they risked being punished by the seniors in the dormitory if they did not.

Students from the more senior classes, especially from Forms Four and above, rarely kept to the rule. In rare instances, the housemaster dropped by to make sure everyone was resting.

The time between the end of the siesta and supper at 6 p.m. was used for various activities. For example, if there was a pending inter-school sporting event, we streamed to the school park to train for the event. Members of the school team could also use the period to train. The same thing applied to members of the school choir. Social activities, such as club meetings, also took place during this period.

During the weekdays, we streamed into our classrooms after the evening meal for prep, which offered us the opportunity to do our homework, revise our notes, read a novel etc.

Prep officially started at 7:00 p.m. when the students were expected to have their heads down poring over their books. It was an offence to disturb the class during prep time. The prep master went round to ensure the rule was adhered to.

The time between the end of supper and the start of the prep period, usually about half an hour (it depended on how long supper lasted), could be described as the period of socialisation and networking.

Was there a female student a boy adored? That was the time he tried to 'knock at her door', so to speak; indeed, to make advances to ascertain whether his affection might be reciprocated!

A *greenhorn* was better advised not to become involved in such matters. If he refused advice and decided to socialise with the opposite sex, he had to tread carefully. How could he know that the female student he was chatting to in the corridors of the classroom block was not the same person a senior student passing by was interested in? Some seniors chose to interrupt the conversation right away by asking the *greenhorn* to either kneel down or hurry to his classroom without delay! Even if a senior student chose not to act immediately, he could 'carry the matter in his head' and mete out a dose of *homoing* to his perceived rival at a later date.

The prep period lasted till 8:45 p.m. for our female counterparts. They were expected to head straight to their dormitories thereafter. Next, ending their prep session at 9:00 p.m., were the boys in Forms One to Three. The final group to head to their dormitories at 9:30 p.m. were male senior students in Forms Four and above.

Every student was expected to be in bed by 10 p.m. when all lights were expected to be off. Students in the junior classes, Forms One to Three, had no choice but to comply. Senior students, namely those in Forms Four and Five as well as the Sixth Formers did not comply strictly to the rule.

-12-
Tidying up for precious points

❖

Saturday morning was time for inspection! That was the time when the senior housemaster went on his rounds through the dormitories to make sure we were maintaining hygiene to the standards of the school.

Starting from Friday afternoon after siesta, each house undertook extensive preparations ahead of the event. Junior students, from Form One to Three were actively involved, the senior students supervising them.

The preparation involved among other things cleaning the floors of the shower room, the toilets, corridors, dormitories as well as the windowsills. All beds were neatly made up in white. Finally, each student also dressed up neatly for the event.

Inspection started at 8:00 a.m. on Saturdays. It was usually not clear where it would start. To be fair to all houses, the starting location was changed from week to week. A few minutes prior to the arrival of the senior housemaster, the housemaster, accompanied by the house captain, came round to quickly undertake a mock inspection, to reassure themselves that everything was in order.

The inspector could award points for tidiness and also deduct points for sub-standard hygiene. Woe betides the student who was found to be directly responsible for causing negative points to be awarded to his/her house! He or she could be punished for the shortcoming. Punishment could involve being assigned a portion of the compound to clear, being called upon to kneel down, to 'pillar', march around, etc.

At the end of the day, the results of the inspection were announced. As might be expected, no house wanted to appear in a bad light by coming last.

Breakfast followed on the heels of inspection on Saturdays. Thereafter those who had been granted a day's exeat to leave the premises of the school could do so. It was strictly forbidden, at any time, to leave the premises of the school without permission. Those who went against the provision risked suspension.

Those who travelled to town were required to comport themselves in a respectable manner. Students were permitted to travel dressed only in their school uniform. Though there were a few other schools in the area, students from each school could be identified by virtue of the school uniform. The public could report the misconduct of a student to the authorities. Serious misdemeanours could lead to sanctions; one could even be suspended from school.

Personally, I rarely found the need to apply for an exeat. I did not have any relations in Oda to visit. For reasons already familiar to the reader, a day's trip to Mpintimpi was out of the question.

Supper on Saturday was followed by an entertainment session which usually began at 7:00 p.m. The session was usually held in the assembly hall. There were various forms of entertainment.

There were times when the dramatic society treated the whole school to a play or drama that they had spent weeks rehearsing. I joined the dramatic society when I was in Form One and remained a member for some time. On a few occasions I played a direct role in such plays.

On other occasions, it was the turn of the debating society to engage in debates about burning and controversial issues of the day. In this case also, the author of these lines played an active role as a member of the debating society.

On some occasions, a film, which had passed the scrutiny of the authorities, was shown. Entry was not free, but highly subsidised.

Then there was what was termed a records night, a form of disco, when we met in the large assembly hall to dance to various music.

On very rare occasions, the school band or even a band from outside, entertained us to live music.

Whatever type of entertainment was arranged for a Saturday, by 10:00 p.m. at the latest it had to come to an end. Under the watchful eyes of the entertainment captain and master, we hurried back to our various dormitories.

-13-
The special Sunday treat

❖

Breakfast on Sundays was quite special. Although we could expect boiled eggs at breakfast on some days of the week, it was a 'never-miss' item at breakfast on Sundays.

Although not compelled to do so, most of us streamed into our classrooms after breakfast on Sunday. That was especially the case when an important examination was around the corner. Some took the opportunity to complete outstanding homework, revise notes, read a novel or engage in other academic activities.

The time between lunch and supper on Sundays was used for recreational activities.

Supper on Sunday evening was followed by Sunday church service. As I mentioned earlier, the part of the country in which I lived could be described as predominantly Christian. There were hardly students of the Muslim faith amongst us. Though, since I was old enough to reason, I have believed in God, at that period in time I could not regard myself as a committed Christian. Nevertheless, I took part wholeheartedly in the service. Indeed, even if I had wanted to stay away, I could not, for attendance was compulsory.

Each student was required to dress in what became known by us as 'white-white' – a white pair of trousers with white shirt and a white coat over the shirt. Each male student was required to wear the school tie.

The service lasted for about 90 minutes. The sermon was usually delivered by a member of the teaching staff. My understanding was that any member of the staff who volunteered to do so could be called upon to assume the role. On a few occasions a guest preacher was in attendance.

-14-

Academic performance and class formation

❖

It was a five-year course that I was engaged in, leading to the GCE 'O'-Level. First year students, also known as Form Ones, were grouped into three classes: 1A, 1B and 1C.

My information was that grouping was based on the results of the common entrance examination. The best 30 formed 1A, the next best 30 1B; the remaining, 1C. We were a little over 100 students in the whole year group.

I was placed in Form 1A, which also came to be known as the 'abemfo' class (the class of brilliant students). The classes were reshuffled at the beginning of each year to reflect the overall performance of the students in the previous academic year.

The following are the subjects we were offered in Form One: English Language, English Literature, Mathematics, General Science, History, Geography, Bible Knowledge (also popularly known as BK), French, Agricultural Science, Music, Arts & Crafts and PE.

It is obvious from the above list that we did not have to learn any local language to begin with. It was in Form Four that one could opt for Twi, the only local language one could offer at the 'O'-Level at Oda.

The above subjects were compulsory for Form One and Two students. In Form Three one had to drop either music or arts & craft.

To obtain a GCE, one had to pass in English, Maths and one science subject as well as four other subjects.

The final subject selection was made at the end of the third year, towards the beginning of the fourth year. Those intending to pursue science-based professions such as medicine, engineering, pharmacy, etc., took that into consideration in their selection. On the other hand those intending to be lawyers, economists, administrators, etc., chose arts subjects.

I had all along dreamt of studying medicine. With that in mind, I decided to select mostly science-based subjects for the 'O'-Level. In the end, I offered the following subjects: English, Mathematics, Additional Mathematics, Physics, Chemistry, Biology, Geography and Economics.

Though I cannot speak for everyone, I can safely say that academic work was taken seriously by the majority of us. We were there not to eat and make merry; we were there to pass our GCEs.

The boarding school environment provided a favourable environment for academic work. In the case of Odasco, the fact that it was situated several kilometres from town and also the fact that means of transportation to travel to town in those days were not easily available, made its location all the more favourable for academic study.

Though a few of us left for town on Saturdays, a good number of us would be found in our classrooms.

Though it was not compulsory, almost every student headed for the classroom on Sundays to revise. Some went there even before breakfast, though most of us went there after.

-15-
Mining for precious nuggets of knowledge

❖

I n a previous chapter I mentioned the fact that all lights in the dormitories were expected to be switched off by 10:00 p.m., and also that all students were expected to be in their beds once the lights were turned off.

When important examinations were pending, students, especially those in the senior classes, sought ways to circumvent the regulation, indeed to stay awake long past the time they were expected to be in bed – in order to revise their notes.

At Oda Secondary, the practice of staying up late into the night to learn for impending examination was known as *mining*. In conventional mining, precious minerals such as silver, gold, diamonds, etc., are extracted from the bedrock. Students at Odasco on their part *mined* through their written notes, textbooks and other literature to extract precious nuggets of knowledge to help them pass their exams.

Some students did their *mining* in the classrooms; others, especially those in the senior classes, did so in the dormitories. Those who *mined* in the dormitories usually resorted to candles as their source of light.

Usually Form One and Two students were not permitted to undertake *mining* 'expeditions', though some considerate house captains occasionally permitted those wishing to do so to stay awake a little past the official bedtime to carry on their venture. Latest by midnight, however, every Form One and Two student who had been granted the permission had to retire to bed.

There were generally no such restrictions on students in senior classes, especially those in Form Four and above. On some occasions, some of them went to the very extreme and stayed awake revising till daybreak! This extreme form of *mining* was referred to as 'from *kenken* to *kankan!*' – a term coined from the Twi language to describe the practice of keeping watch overnight.

Starting from Form Three when there were not many restrictions on me to keep the bedtime rule, I engaged regularly in *mining*. Usually I stayed awake till around midnight, though on a few occasions I persevered till around 3 o'clock in the morning. Much as I tried, however, I hardly ever made it to 'from *kenken* to *kankan*'.

Mining, as I have just mentioned, was the expression we used for the practice of staying awake deep into the night to revise for an impending examination. Various terms were coined in various schools in the country to describe the actual attempt by the student to memorize notes prior to an examination. At Odasco, the popular expressions in use were: 'chewing baba' and 'chewing apow'. Thus, when students spoke of their attempt to 'chew baba' or 'chew apow' they meant they were leaving no stone unturned in their attempt to learn their notes by heart ahead of an impending examination. Others also spoke of trying to 'chew pour pass and forget!'

Personally, I did not take any chances when it came to preparing for examinations. Usually I started with my revision several weeks ahead of the impending event. During the week the prep sessions offered a good opportunity to reread my notes. On Saturdays and Sundays, I vanished into the classroom after breakfast, and remained there until after supper when I left for the Saturday evening entertainment session or Sunday evening worship service as the case might be.

I usually always had a guilty conscience when I saw others absorbed in their books whilst I was engaged in something else. Even if I had just before spent several hours doing so myself, I still thought I was not doing enough compared to some of my mates, the likes, for example, of Robert Mensah, da Costa and Agbenyegah!

My good friend Robert Mensah! Whenever an important examination was pending, he seemed to be occupied with his books around the clock! At least that was the impression he made not only on me but several of his other classmates. Even after he had spent several hours in the classroom revising and he finally decided to leave for the dormitory, he could not dispense with his notes – not even during the short walk to the dormitory, about 200 metres away. Instead one could spot him holding a notebook or textbook close before his eyes and intensely absorbed with it as he walked!

-16-
'www.exams-need-to-be-passed.com'

A s I write these recollections of my secondary school experience in January 2014, information technology has made great advances and taken hold of society. Mobile phones, smart phones, laptops, notebooks, iPods, iPads, etc., are everywhere.

When I began my second-cycle education in September 1971, the only means of communication available to me and my peers was by way of letter writing. Though elsewhere in the world communication by way of the telephone was the norm, the telephone line at the disposal of the school was only for official use; while it was also in the homes of the teaching staff, there was no public phone on the school compound where a student could call his/her relatives. Even if that were the case, it would have meant nothing to me, for my parents at little Mpintimpi had no access to any of the modern facilities of that period – no phones, no electricity, no tap water. When I left home for school, they had no idea when I would return. I just surprised them with my arrival for the mid-term and end-of-term holidays.

During a visit to Odasco in 2013, the headmaster spoke about the dilemma the school authorities faced on the issue of mobile phones. Should they allow students to bring them to school or not?

In the end they decided to ban them. Though they were officially not allowed on the premises, he conceded that not a few students still managed to smuggle them in. He reported several instances when the authorities had to deal with issues and incidents – fights, bullying, crimes – related to the devices.

I am not asking for the clock of time to be turned backwards, to take us back to those days when we could concentrate on our books without the temptation to be distracted by the opportunities of modern technology. The student should realise, however, that modern technology or not, the need to pass exams and to compete in a modern world has not changed.

-17-
Boys behaving gentlemanly only in the presence of girls

❖

I n this chapter I shall dwell on matters relating to one of the most important meeting places of the student population – the dining hall.

Usually a student was assigned to the same dining table throughout a particular academic year. About 20 students were assigned to each table. Nine students sat on each side of the long table facing each other. The table head, who was responsible for order and discipline at the table, sat at the head of the table whilst the assistant table head occupied the other end.

The seating arrangement was by way of houses. The fact that it was a mixed-sex boarding school was reflected in the seating arrangement – the sexes were not separated from each other but usually sat alongside each other, a female student, then a male, then a female until the row was full.

Though, I cannot speak for everyone, the male students behaved in a gentlemanly fashion as long as our female counterparts were present. The moment the session was officially dismissed and some of the male students remained behind to 'take care' of food still left untouched, the decorum usually ceased.

-18-
Face-to-face with a peculiar dining custom and culture

❖

I was introduced to a completely different dining custom and culture at the boarding school. The food there was very different to what I had been used to.

At Mpintimpi almost every resident of the village was engaged in small-scale farming. Two different types of crops were cultivated. The first category consisted of cash crops. The second category comprised crops destined for our own consumption. We literally grew what we ate and ate what we grew.

Among the crops meant for consumption were plantain, yams, cocoyams, cassava, maize – all carbohydrates – as well as vegetables such as garden eggs, kidney beans, groundnuts, tomatoes, onions, etc.

Even when it came to cooking oil, the villagers relied on their own produce instead of factory-made cooking oil. The two main types of cooking oil we had recourse to were palm oil, which is gleaned from the flesh of the palm oil fruit, and palm kernel oil, which is made from the seed embedded in the nut of the palm oil fruit.

It was only when it came to meat or fish that the villagers could not claim complete self-sufficiency. Though they provided part of their meat requirements through fishing in the nearby Nwi River and also by laying traps to catch bush meat, on several occasions we were forced to resort to the dry fish offered for sale by market mamas who travelled far to the coast to acquire their wares.

What then was the typical daily menu of residents of Mpintimpi? Breakfast was usually *ampesi*, that is boiled plantain or yams plus a sauce; lunch was also *ampesi*, whereas supper was *fufu* (pounded plantain and cassava with soup to go with it). That was what I had been used to all my life growing up in little Mpintimpi.

Cocoa was the main cash crop produced by the residents of Mpintimpi. We were taught at school that among the products made from cocoa were chocolate, cocoa butter, beverages, etc. As far as we were concerned, that comprised meals for the rest of the world, but not ourselves.

At Odasco, the poor village boy was required not only to eat with a set of cutlery but was also introduced to 'European' breakfasts, which included tea, coffee and cocoa beverages (as the case may be) served with white bread, with butter, margarine, orange jam or peanut butter!

Various forms of porridge – k*oko* (porridge from cornmeal), *rice water* (rice porridge) and *Tom Brown* were also on the menu.

How the porridge prepared from the meal of roasted maize came to be known as *Tom Brown* remains a mystery to me to this day! In the end it became one of my favourite items on the breakfast menu.

On one or two occasions during the week, we were served hard-boiled eggs at breakfast.

The above combination, that is beverages and/or porridge with bread and various kinds of spreads, might be described as constituting our standard breakfast.

It was interrupted only on Saturdays when we were usually served *'yo ke garri'*. For the sake of those unfamiliar with it, *'yo ke garri'* is a combination of boiled brown kidney beans and sauce made of palm oil or palm kernel oil eaten with *garri*.

Lunch was usually made up of boiled plantain, yams or rice with various kinds of sauce to go with – *nkontomire*.

For most of us our favourite lunch, without doubt, was what we called 'red-red'! For the sake of readers not conversant with the meal, I shall offer a brief description.

Plantain is originally green; as it ripens it turns yellow and assumes a sweeter flavour. To prepare 'red-red' the yellow skin is peeled from the ripened plantain. The ripened plantain is then fried in cooking oil for a while and served with a sauce, usually made from kidney beans. Though the fried plantain can be eaten with any sauce, the typical 'red-red' is eaten with the kidney beans sauce.

'Red-red' was not only my favourite, but that of almost every student. Unless prevented by ill health or other unforeseeable circumstances, hardly any student missed a meal of 'red-red'.

Supper did not differ much from lunch and consisted of rice, boiled yams, kenkey and various kinds of sauce to go with it.

Another aspect of boarding school life that differed from what I was used to was that the meals were regular – breakfast, lunch, dinner – served almost at the same time each day.

At Mpintimpi we did not follow any strict regime for eating our meals – we just ate when we got hungry! If I had an urge to eat four or five times during the day and the food was available, I just did so. If on other occasions, we had to leave home early for work on the farm, we did so without first thinking about taking our meals. We went about our duties until mother cooked something for us around midday. On our return home in the evening, we ate the last meal of the day – *fufu*.

-19-

Yearning for the familiar fufu-balls

❖

W e were expected to turn up punctually for our meals. That wasn't usually a problem during weekdays.

It was another matter at weekends when, for various reasons, some of us turned up late for meals. Others on the table, thinking that perhaps a latecomer was not going to come, wasted no time in sharing the 'surplus' food. Sometimes the latecomer did indeed stay away. On other occasions, however, the latecomer turned up – to find his/her plate empty!

'Where is my food?' he/she would inquire. As might be expected, everyone kept quiet.

Perhaps it was selfishness on our part; the fact remains, however, that we, the male students, generally expected the female students to stay away from the dining hall at weekends, especially on Saturdays. Consequently, some of us made derogatory remarks aimed at the female students who turned up for meals at weekends, especially on Saturdays. Though we did not say it to their faces, behind their backs we called them all sorts of names.

The reader might ask if there was any meal that I detested. For the benefit of those unfamiliar with the diverse composition of the population of my native Ghana, let me explain that it is made up several tribes. Some of these tribes speak languages that differ completely from one another. So, as might be expected, the meals of such diverse population groups differ from one another.

For example, *kenkey,* prepared from fermented maize dough, is the favourite meal of the Gas and Fantis population groups that dwell mainly in southern Ghana, along the Atlantic coast. There are two main types of *kenkey*: *Ga* and *Fanti kenkey*. As the name implies, *Ga kenkey* is eaten mainly by the Gas whereas *Fanti kenkey* is eaten mainly by the Fantis. During my childhood days, though mother occasionally prepared a version of *Fanti kenkey*, it was meant mainly for sale, not for home consumption.

As I mentioned earlier, our boarding school did not serve only the children of a certain catchment area; rather, it was open to children of the whole country. During our schooldays quite a considerable number of our students came from the *Ga, Ewe* and *Fanti* regions of the country.

To be fair to all, the school did not serve meals that were acceptable only to the local population but also to those from other parts of the country. Thus *kenkey*, both the *Fanti* and *Ga* varieties, were a regular feature on our menu – they were offered at least twice a week. Those were the occasions when I yearned for mother's kitchen! Indeed, even to this day, I struggle to get a meal of *kenkey* down my throat.

Was there any meal I missed and longed for at the boarding school? Certainly there was! As I have already mentioned, *fufu* was our main evening meal at Mpintimpi. Whoever has visited the area in Ghana where I grew up would become familiar with the *pum-pum* sound that emanates from the homes of residents in the evenings. It is indeed the time of day that *fufu* is pounded! A meal of *fufu* has two main components: the *fufu* balls and the soup to go with it. The balls are obtained through a laborious process of pounding boiled cassava together with either plantain or cocoyam.

If for any reason, Mother was not able to prepare a meal of *fufu* on a particular day, she considered herself as having fasted for the day, never mind if she had filled her stomach with something else. I must add that she was not alone in her attitude. Indeed, for many an individual residing in that part of the world a meal of *fufu* is considered just as essential to life as oxygen and water!

I missed *fufu*. Naturally, I did not expect the school to go to the lengths required in providing us with a meal that involves quite elaborate preparation.

Before I leave this chapter on matters of the stomach I should mention that, on a few occasions during my schooldays, tension arose between the school population on the one hand and the school authorities on the other. Indeed, despite all the efforts of the school authorities to provide adequate and good quality food for the students, there were times when there was displeasure concerning the quality and quantity of the food. I'll return to this issue later in my narration.

-20-
Our headmaster and his oversized pair of trousers

❖

M r Amissah-Arthur, enshrined in our memories, was the headmaster. He was a lovely and likeable middle-aged man. I cannot say for certain how old he was at the time of my admission to Odasco, but my guess is he was about 55.

The topography of Odasco was predominantly flat. A few hillocks interrupted the flat topography. Was it by design, so as to give our headmaster a panoramic view of what was happening at his school at any time? Or was it just coincidence?

Whatever the reason, the fact is that the headmaster's residence happened to occupy a strategic location on the compound, being situated on the most prominent and elevated part that overlooked the entire school premises.

He was a lovely and likeable personality. I found out on my arrival at the school that in previous years he had been engaged in teaching. At the time of my arrival his role was mainly administrative. As a result, he was rarely seen. He only appeared before morning assembly to address the school on important occasions

Students, students, students! Despite the fact that he was such a decent person, we sought and found a way to make fun of him. In the end we settled on his pair of trousers! He seemed always to wear a pair of oversized trousers – that in any case was the impression he made on us, for whenever he stood before us to address us, he, at short intervals of time, took hold of the waist of his trousers and pulled it upwards. We thought he did so to prevent it from sliding downwards!

Several years after I had left the walls of Odasco, he retired to live in his home town Cape Coast, a coastal city about 100 kilometres to the west of Accra (more about Cape Coast later). He has in the meantime been called to eternity. May his soul rest in perfect peace.

-21-
Different staple foods in different settings

❖

M r Abosi, the assistant headmaster, was about the same age as the headmaster or perhaps a few years younger. He was a man with a great sense of humour. He became our geography teacher in Form Three. We all looked forward to his class, not so much because of the love we had for geography, but because of the jokes that he was so fond of cracking!

Once during a lesson on the corn belt of the US he stated:

'Maize is the staple food for cattle in the US.' He paused for a while to look around the class, then continued: 'Let me repeat what I said. In the US maize is the staple food for cattle. Well, as you are all aware, in Ghana it is the staple food of the ethnic groups residing along the coast.' He paused again to take a look around the class.

'Are there any members of such tribes in the class?' he asked.

A few hands went up.

'Well,' he continued with a twinkle in his eye, 'if we follow this line of logic, one might surmise that you have the same status as cattle!'

Looks of disbelief and bewilderment were exchanged round the class.

-22-
The minister for stomach affairs

❖

M r Donkor, also referred to as 'Kwaadonkor' by many a student, was the music teacher for the whole school. He was also in charge of the school choir. Much as the above roles would probably have been enough to make his face familiar to most students, it was indeed, another position he had that made him one of the most familiar staff member present. 'Kwaadonkor', in short, was also the dining hall master.

The position of the dining hall master was one of the hottest seats to occupy. Indeed, as far as we students were concerned, apart from the headmaster, no other position was as important.

On not a few occasions he had to rush to the dining hall to appease irate and hungry students, who, despite being hungry, were refusing to accept their meals for reasons of either poor quality, insufficient quantity or both! (I will return to this issue at a later stage in my narration.)

Because of his position as the dining hall master some of us, having no basis or foundation in fact, described him as a *food-lover*. I personally did not share that opinion.

-23-
Mr Mese Bu!

I n Form Four one of my subjects was mathematics or what was also known as additional mathematics.

Mr Asiedu was our additional mathematics teacher. He also taught us physics. He was a very correct and dedicated teacher. He had a way of saying, 'Do you understand?'

A few of us, on some occasions, seemed to create the impression of being even more knowledgeable than our esteemed mathematics master. On other occasions some of us just wanted to ask questions or make comments to irritate or provoke him.

'Hey, my friend, do you think you know better than everyone else? If that's the case, *mese bu*! (*you* solve the problem!)'

Several years after I left Odasco, he was promoted to the position of assistant headmaster.

Our history teacher and the zip that refused to 'shut up!'

❖

O ur history teacher in Form Three had a great passion for his subject. He did not just *teach* a subject, he literally *preached* it! Even if the subject was 'dry' he presented it in a way that made it lively. Indeed it was never boring in his class.

As I mentioned earlier, the class formation was based on academic performance. That was the case until the end of the third year. Thereafter, one was assigned to a class based on subject combinations.

It was not my intention to say anything about gender differences. The fact remains, however, that in our case, the make-up of the A class was about 80 per cent male and 20 per cent female.

As far as I recall the seating arrangement in the class was not imposed on us from above. It was rather the choice of our female counterparts to occupy the first few front seats of each row. Thus it happened that in each classroom one visited, female students were mostly in the front while their male counterparts were at the back.

One day, during the Form Three history lesson class, our 'preacher' teacher was enthusiastically presenting his 'message' for the day when I became aware from my position in the middle row of some murmuring going on among the girls in the front seats each time our teacher turned his back on the class to write something on the board.

Then, mid-way through the lesson, all of a sudden, Eva, a slender girl of fair complexion, got out of her seat and approached our teacher who was delivering his material with enthusiasm. What was she up to, I wondered?

Our teacher probably thought she was approaching him to seek his permission to leave the classroom to attend a call of nature, for he signalled his permission for her to leave. That, however, was apparently not the case, for she drew closer to him instead of heading for the door. Finally, she whispered something into his ear.

The demeanour of our teacher changed immediately. Clearly embarrassed, he turned his back to the class and quickly zipped up his fly before turning to us to continue his 'lecture'.

As it turned out, the zip of his trousers had been open all the time he stood in front of us delivering his 'lecture'. By dint of their prominent position in the front row, the girls had noticed the problem very early into the lesson. It took a while, however, for Eva to muster the courage to draw his attention to the problem; certainly none of the other girls had the courage to do so!

As might be expected, the room remained tense during the remaining minutes. No sooner had our teacher left the room, than the whole class burst into uncontrollable laughter. For the next several minutes we laughed our hearts out.

'You girls! You did enjoy the spectacle, didn't you!?' one of us exclaimed.

'What makes you say that?" our female counterparts hit back as if in one voice.

'Why didn't you notify him immediately instead of waiting for ages!'

'We just didn't have the courage to do so!' they admitted.

-25-
Mr 'Make-sure-you-are-not-caught!'

◆

Historians tell us that in November 1884 the imperial chancellor of the German Empire, Otto von Bismarck, convened a conference of 14 states (including the United States) to settle the political partitioning of Africa. At the conference in Berlin, the whole continent of Africa was arbitrarily partitioned among the imperial powers of the time. Of these 14 nations, France, Germany, Great Britain, and Portugal were the major players in the conference, controlling most of colonial Africa at the time. The borders were drawn arbitrarily without taking into consideration the ethnicity of the inhabitants living there.

As a result of the arbitrary partitioning of Africa, Ghana, a former English colony, is now sandwiched between three French-speaking countries to the north, east and west. Only God knows which European country would have been apportioned the area to the south of Ghana, had it not been for the presence of the Atlantic Ocean – the Portuguese perhaps?

Ghana, formerly the Gold Coast, was until 6 March 1957 a British colony. As I write, English is still the official language. It is superfluous to mention that English was a compulsory subject at the secondary school level.

From what I have just mentioned, it comes as no surprise that French is the second European language apart from English that is widely taught in schools in Ghana.

At Odasco, it was compulsory for every student to study French up till Form Three. In Form One, initially our French teacher was a

Ghanaian national who had been teaching at Odasco for some time. In the course of the first term, he was assigned to one of the senior classes.

In his place a new French teacher, who happened to be a citizen of Burkina Faso, formerly the Upper Volta, Ghana's direct neighbour to the north, took over the Form One French class. As it turned out, Odasco happened to be his first posting after being recruited directly from his native country by the Ghana Education Service.

As I just mentioned, our previous French teacher was a Ghanaian national. As might be expected from a Ghanaian citizen with his academic background, he also had a good command of the English language. Besides that, he also spoke Twi. During the French class, he resorted to either English or Twi to explain a point we had difficulty grasping.

In contrast to our ex-French teacher, our new French teacher had hardly any knowledge of English. The stage was thus set for the problems that ensued between our French teacher on the one hand and the class on the other.

Bubbling with energy and high enthusiasm for his job, our stoutly built and highly tempered new French teacher went about his duty with committed diligence.

In his enthusiasm – perhaps over-enthusiasm – to teach us the official language of his country, he seemed to have lost sight of the fact that he was dealing with novices in the language. That in any case, was the impression he gave us whenever he stood before us and, like a parrot, screeched out his incomprehensible vocabulary.

The class on its part sat still and stared at him. The silence on our part did not prevail for long, though! Whenever our zealous, perhaps overzealous, teacher turned his back to the class to write something on the blackboard, some of us took advantage of the situation and vented our frustration in various ways – mimicking, gesticulating wildly, making noises, chatting, etc.

Sometimes, he turned round to catch some of us red handed in the act. Making use of the little knowledge of English at his command, he sternly warned the culprits to either behave or face the consequences if he caught anyone misbehaving the next time. To quote his own words, he warned everyone to 'Make *sure you are not caught, Satan laws!'*

The practical implication of his warning was that if anyone was caught by him, that person would be the subject of his immediate and decisive retribution. Indeed, without any further ado, our well-built teacher made straight for the next offender. Making use of his fist or a ruler as the case might be, he gave the wrongdoer a knock or hit on the head.

Was it due to the improvement of his knowledge of English on his part and ours regarding some progress in our knowledge of French that led eventually to better communication between him and us? In any case, as time went on we gradually got on quite well with him. Though he did not depart from his trademark policy of: '*Make sure you are not caught, Satan laws!*' he did not practically enforce it as frequently as he used to in the initial stages.

I had to bear with him until the end of the third academic year when I dropped French. To be fair to him, my decision to drop that subject had more to do with my personal future plans than his personality and style.

George, my best friend at Odasco, on his part selected French for his 'O'-Level and had to bear with him for two further years. According to him, our energetic and sometimes turbulent teacher mellowed even further with time and, in the end, became one of his favourite teachers.

-26-
The palm wine tapper from the USA!

❖

The teaching staff was made up mostly of Ghanaians. As in the case of our temperamental French teacher from Burkina Faso, there were also a few expatriate teachers on the teaching staff. They came from various parts of the world – other African countries, India, Pakistan and the United States.

The expatriate teachers from the United States came as part of the Peace Corps programme. The majority of them returned home at the end of their posting. Not so Mr Thorne, who was head of the Physics Department in our time. During his stay in Ghana he met and married a Ghanaian woman.

In the course of time he became what one might describe as an 'Africanised American'. Not only did he master the local Twi language, he was at home also when it came to the local meals. My understanding was that he was capable even of tapping palm wine. For those not conversant with the process, I shall provide a brief explanation.

Palm wine is obtained by tapping the oil palm tree. Usually the tapper first has to fell the entire tree before tapping can take place, though some tappers do collect the sap from the cut flower of the still standing palm tree. During the first few days of tapping, the white liquid that collects is sweet and free of alcohol. The sweet alcohol-free sap is scorned by many a lover of palm wine, regarding it as a drink for women and children.

With the help of atmospheric and also residual yeast left in the collecting container, palm sap begins to ferment shortly after collection.

Within hours, fermentation yields an aromatic wine of up to four percent alcohol content. The wine may be allowed to ferment for longer, up to a day, to yield a stronger, more sour and acidic taste, something preferred by the seasoned palm wine drinker.

Whereas European and American visitors usually prefer to purchase their palm wine from local vendors, our American 'turned' Ghanaian member of staff chose in the end to tap the palm trees himself!

Mr Thorne our physics teacher became so integrated into native society that, but for the colour of his skin, one might have regarded him as a native!

-27-
The school authorities attempt to paint a beautiful picture of our school

❖

O nce a year the school held a speech and prize-giving day. The open day offered the general public, in particular parents, the opportunity to acquaint themselves with the activities of the school.

On such a special occasion when the attention of the world was focussed on the school, one might expect the authorities would go to great lengths in their efforts to show the school in a good light. That was exactly what happened. Various departments of the school, in particular the Science, Music as well as the Art and Craft Department, held exhibitions to mark the occasion. Cultural as well as theatrical displays were also enacted to entertain the public.

The attempt of the authorities to paint a favourable picture of the school was reflected also in the meals served in the dining hall on the special day. From breakfast to lunch all the way to supper, the kitchen went to great lengths to provide not only good quality meals but also an abundance of everything on offer.

As the name implies, it was a day not only for the general public to familiarise themselves with the activities of the school, but also a day of 'speeches' and the awarding of prizes. Every year the school invited an individual of high standing in society – the Minister of Education, the Regional Minister, a leading academic, a successful businessman or businesswoman, etc. – as the guest of honour. The duty fell on the chosen individual to deliver the main speech of the day.

The main event of the day – speeches and the presentation of prizes – got under way around 3 p.m. in the main assembly hall. After the school choir had entertained the gathering with a rendition of some of the best songs from their repertoire, and the drama society had entertained the guests to the best performances from their range, came the climax of the occasion: the delivering of speeches and the distribution of the prizes.

The first speaker would always be the headmaster. In a speech lasting about half an hour he would present to the gathering a picture of the main occurrences or developments of the school during the preceding year.

The climax of the events of the day was the address of the guest speaker. Irrespective of his/her social, religious, political background, the core message of the distinguished guest sought to exhort us among other things to be dedicated to our books, to be obedient to the school authority and to shun anything that could stand before us and our academic performance.

The address of the guest speaker was followed by the presentation of prizes – in the main, book prizes. Prizes were awarded in various categories, among others, the best student in each year group, the best student in each subject of a year group, the best house captain, the tidiest house, etc.

One might ask whether the author of these lines ever won a prize. The answer is in the affirmative. I do not, however, wish to go into details, to avoid being accused of trying to blow my own trumpet before the whole world! Whoever wishes to have further details in the matter is welcome to consult the school records.

-28-
Bananas and peanuts needed to fine-tune voices

❖

D uring my time at Odasco the school boasted a choir of distinction. The school choir entertained us to uplifting and beautiful music, not only during Sunday church services, but also during the speech and prize giving day. On a few occasions the choir was even invited to perform outside the school.

Indeed, I would have liked to be a member of the school choir. As might be expected, I could not just turn up and register to be a member. Instead those wishing to do so had to undergo a voice test. After careful thought, I decided not to give it a try in order to save myself from embarrassment. Our choirmaster on hearing my coarse voice, which could not be classified in any of the standard male voice registers – countertenor, tenor, baritone, or bass – would, without doubt, have shown me to the door without much deliberation.

There were a few members of the school choir both in my class and dormitory. On one occasion, the following conversation ensued between me and one of them:

'Whenever we report for a practice session, we are made to eat some bananas and peanuts, before we begin with the practice,' my mate began.

'Why so?' I inquired, surprised.

'Eating bananas and peanuts shortly before singing is said to lead to an improvement in voice quality!' he explained.

'Really?'

'Well, that's what we are told by our choirmaster. Initially I was sceptical. Now I can also testify to that!'

'Then the next time I report for a voice test I'll eat some bananas and peanuts!' I smiled.

'I don't think that will make any difference in your case', my advisor said. 'One should have a good voice to begin with! The bananas and peanuts only help for fine-tuning!'

-29-

Combing dormitories in search of lost clothing

❖

T he school had a laundry facility. It was not for free; laundry fees were part of the boarding fees.

One could present only the prescribed components of the school uniform for washing. To prevent uniforms from going missing, each of us was required to write our names with indelible ink on the inside labels of the pieces of clothing involved.

The dirty linen was deposited at a collection point of each house and taken to the laundry by selected Form One students on Mondays. The washed and neatly ironed items were ready for collection on Friday afternoons.

In just the same way that the dirty clothing was not submitted on an individual basis, so the washed items were not collected on an individual basis. Instead they were collected by selected Form One students from each house and deposited at designated areas of the various houses for collection by their owners.

Though it was not a common occurrence, there were times when items went missing. The first thing one did when this happened was to go from house to house to look for the missing item(s). With some luck, one might find it mixed up with those of a different house.

There were instances, though, when the search proved futile – the item involved will have simply vanished. One could not get the school to replace lost items; one had to turn to one's parents/guardians to do so. On the whole, however, the system functioned quite well, and losses were exceptions rather than the rule.

It is perhaps unnecessary to mention here that we had to wash items of our underwear ourselves. Most of us used the time between breakfast and lunch or the time between lunch and supper on Saturdays to handwash them. We then hung them on several drying lines in a large open space behind our dormitory building, erected by the school for this purpose. The generous African sun usually facilitated rapid drying.

A Form One student could, throughout the academic year, be called upon by a senior student, usually those in Form Four and beyond to help wash some clothes – underwear included.

-30-
Contract cleaning firms unwanted!

✦

E lsewhere in our world, authorities hire special hands to clean the school compound. During my secondary school days, the duty of cleaning the school – the classrooms, the dormitories and the compound at large – fell upon the student population.

Earlier in my narration I touched on the weekly inspection regime. Cleaning of the dormitory was not restricted to Saturdays only. Throughout the week students were responsible for cleaning the dormitories as well as the immediate surroundings of the dormitory blocks.

It was also the responsibility of students to tidy the classrooms.

The duty of tidying the school usually fell upon students in Forms One to Three. Students in the senior classes, from Forms Four and Five as well as Lower and Upper Six, were exempt from such activities.

To ensure an orderly course of events, duty rosters were made up that assigned the role to various students on a weekly basis.

-31-

The mock parliament of Odasco

❖

The school council was a student representative body that liaised between the student population on the one hand and the school authorities on the other.

Usually, one could channel minor grievances to the class captain who, in turn, passed them on to the teacher responsible for the class.

On matters relating to the dormitory, grievances could be brought to the attention of the house captain. The captain could choose to resolve the issue or pass it on to the housemaster/mistress as the case may be.

The School Council was made up of representatives chosen from classes, houses, as well as the overall School Prefect, the Girls' Prefect and a few other senior students. It concerned itself with issues affecting the welfare of the student population in general – issues relating to academic performance, standard of the food served in the dining hall, attitude of staff towards students, etc.

Decisions taken at council meetings were brought to the attention of the headmaster. He could decide to act on them alone or involve his staff.

-32-
Aluta continua!

◆

As I pointed out in the previous chapter, there were various channels through which students could make their grievances heard. Despite that arrangement, unfortunately, there were times when students, be it a minority or majority of the school population, felt their grievances were either not addressed at all or were not properly addressed and who held demonstrations to get their grievances rectified. I must add here that usually the main cause for dissatisfaction revolved around the school meals – either the protestors were unhappy with the quantity, the quality or both. Such student demonstration against perceived injustices by the school authorities came to be known as *aluta*.

Though initially meant to be peaceful, protests, in most cases, turned violent, with resultant damage to school property and, in some cases, even the health of the demonstrators, teaching staff or both parties.

In trying to vent their anger at a perceived injustice on the side of the authorities, some of us vented our anger against school property, leading to destruction and vandalism of school property – furniture, glass windows, buildings, school vehicles, etc.

Though demonstrations never went to that extreme during my time at Odasco, there were occasional reports of demonstrations turning very violent, leading for example to the burning of the school bus.

In a few instances, some demonstrators even went to the extent of assaulting members of staff. As might be expected, the headmaster was usually their prime target. Other targets were the assistant headmaster, the dining hall master, the senior housemaster and the various housemasters/housemistresses.

Such demonstrations led in some instances to the closure of the school for a while, though not during my time at the school.

The ring leaders of such protests risked being suspended from school for a considerable period of time. In some cases they were even expelled from school altogether.

Such individuals risked a premature end to their academic career for, as might be expected, hardly any headteacher was prepared to admit someone who had been expelled from another school for misconduct.

Aluta demonstrations were not limited to second-cycle schools. Universities and other institutions of higher learning were open to forms of protest from time to time. On a few occasions university students in Ghana embarked on *aluta* to demand a return to civilian rule.

-33-
The silent pianos of Odasco

As I mentioned earlier, when we got to Form Three we were required to offer either music or arts & craft as part of our curriculum. Arts & craft being my weakest subject, I readily dropped it without much consideration.

It would amount to exaggeration or hyperbole if I were to claim here that I possessed the genius of a Mozart or a Beethoven! I do believe, however, that given the opportunity I might at least have acquired the ability to play the piano.

The ability to acquire such a skill however was handicapped, since the school did not possess the basic instrument to practice with – apart from the piano mentioned below, which was not accessible to students!

Our music teacher (readers might recall he was also our dining hall master) did his best to impart his knowledge to his students. There was one major handicap though – as far as my memory goes, our school possessed only one large piano. It was fixed on the podium of our assembly hall. One would not expect the school authorities to allow novices like me to practise on the single piano of the entire school. That indeed was the case.

How then did we practise playing the piano or the organ in our music class? Our music teacher could be described as inventive. He called upon each student of his class to construct a replica of the keyboard making use of wood or cardboard as well as black and white paint. In the end, each one of us constructed what we referred to as a 'silent piano' measuring about 70cm in length and 30cm in breadth.

With the help of our improvised keyboards we went about practising how to play various hymns! During lessons, our dutiful music master went round the class, to make sure each student was playing the correct keys of the tune being practised!

We not only practised on our silent piano during lessons; we were also given homework that we were required to practise in our various dormitories ahead of the next music lesson.

We learnt to play several hymns. One of them – 'Oh God our help in ages past, our hope for years to come!' – has remained one of my favourites to this day!

-34-
The call of nature becomes a social event

❖

E ach dormitory block was equipped with a few water closets or flush toilets. Considering the number of boarders in each dormitory, it is not surprising that they turned out to be insufficient. To get round the problem the authorities constructed a pit latrine for the male students. It was located about five minutes' walk from the classroom blocks.

Though students from the junior classes, especially Forms One to Three were not prevented from using the WC, they resorted to the pit latrine whenever convenient. This was to avoid the situation where they could clash with senior students also desirous of using the facility.

I do not know when the term *Alapo* was first coined to describe our pit latrine. Neither am I aware who first invented the term. The fact is that when I arrived at Odasco the term had gained universal usage among the student population – including our female counterparts.

A visit to the *Alapo* eventually became a kind of 'social event'. Indeed, unless the call of nature was very urgent, hardly any one of us made the *trip* to the *Alapo* alone. What usually happened was that the individual experiencing the first signs of the need to empty the bowels made the situation known to friends or nearby mates.

Could the call of nature be contagious? Well, I'm inclined to believe that it is, at least based on the curious experience I had at Odasco. Indeed, no sooner had one of my mates made his intention to visit the *Alapo* known than I, too, experienced the urge to follow suit!

-35-
Students turned paramedics

❖

The school boasted a small dispensary. It was stocked with medication for treating common conditions such as headaches, malaria, diarrhoea and vomiting. One could also go there for first aid in case of minor injuries.

There was no resident nurse; a student from one of the senior classes was entrusted with the running of the dispensary for a particular academic year. I cannot say for sure what criteria were used to select such an individual.

Students with conditions that could not be handled at the dispensary had to attend the district hospital at Oda. During weekdays, students needing to go there left the school premises after breakfast with the school bus. Usually, the group returned to school in time for lunch.

Though it rarely happened, there were a few medical emergencies that necessitated students being rushed to hospital.

One such emergency requiring transport to hospital involved me personally. I was having a shower when I slipped and fell on my face. In the process, one of my front teeth of the upper jaw got cracked. I also suffered deep cut wounds to my gum. In terrible pain with blood gushing from my mouth, I headed for the dispensary. After I had received some pain killers, I was taken to hospital for further treatment. My prayer as the vehicle sped towards the hospital was that my injury would not be deemed serious enough to be admitted. And so it happened. After examining the root of the cracked tooth and determining that it did not need to be extracted I was given pain killers and sent back to school.

Over the next few days I had to endure the quite severe pain resulting from the broken tooth.

The gap resulting from the half-broken tooth widened a few years later when I fell again and broke the good neighbour of the already broken tooth!

The gap was closed by a zealous German dentist when I moved to Germany.

-36-
Chicken and poxes spread misery and anguish

❖

When I got to Form Three all of a sudden, several students began, simultaneously, to complain of headaches, general bodily aches and of generally feeling unwell.

Initially those affected thought they had caught malaria – an infectious disease caused by the plasmodium parasite, which is transmitted from person to person through mosquitoes; no wonder, for in our part of the world malaria is so endemic it is the first thought that usually comes to the minds of residents when they develop a fever.

Initially those affected consulted the school dispensary where they were given paracetamol. The medication, however, brought only temporary relief.

Not long after the onset of the symptoms outlined above, those affected began to develop an itchy rash. Initially the rash affected a few areas of the body, but in time it began to spread – behind the ears, on the face, the scalp, under the arm, the chest and belly, the arms and legs – in short, from head to toe! For some the rash spread even inside the ears and mouth!

In time the rash that began as small, itchy red spots, turned into blisters and became intensely itchy. What began as afflicting only a few among us began to spread to the entire school community.

Eventually, those affected were sent to the Oda District Hospital. What some of us had in the meantime begun to suspect was confirmed by the medical experts – the medical condition known as chicken pox!

It is superfluous to state here that chicken pox is a highly contagious disease. Within days of the appearance of the first symptoms of the disease on the school premises, it had spread to a considerable proportion of the student population, both male and female.

Initially, the rumours made the rounds that the authorities were considering closing down the school and sending the students home. In the end – probably considering that we would spread the disease further in the community if we were sent home – they decided against the idea.

Two makeshift isolation stations were created to house those affected. As far as the male students were concerned, the second floor of the science block, which was about 200 metres away from the dormitory buildings, served as our 'isolation ward'. In the case of the female population the isolation station was in the vicinity of the female dormitory.

During my childhood and boyhood days at Mpintimpi, I was victim to all kinds of ailments – malaria, measles, diarrhoea, vomiting, etc. Up to the time of the outbreak at Odasco, however, I had been spared chicken pox. When, after more than a week into the outbreak, I was still not showing any symptoms of the disease, I thought I would escape the ordeal. That soon turned out to be wishful thinking.

One day, not long after the outbreak had been officially confirmed and the isolation facility had been set up, I returned from lessons feeling generally unwell. Soon I began to feel feverish. As if that were not enough, my head and all my joints began to ache badly. Soon my whole body began to shake violently.

'Friend, hurry to the dispensary and get your temperature checked!' one of my classmates advised me.

Soon I was on my way. Quite a number of us, all displaying symptoms similar to mine, had already lined up at the door by the time I got there. After standing in the queue for about half an hour, it came to my turn for my temperature to be taken. 38.9 degrees Celsius, the thermometer recorded my temperature. Not only that, the dispenser detected a few spots on my body.

'You have caught the chicken pox!' the student in charge of the dispensary confirmed. 'Go straight to the isolation ward. I will send someone to notify your house captain about your condition.' He continued: 'We will also arrange for one of your classmates to deposit items of clothing and hygiene at the collection point on the isolation ward.'

And so I became a member of the community of the isolated. At the time I joined them, the number had soared to around 50 students.

Although several years have since elapsed, I still recall the terribly itchy rash associated with the disease. To provide some relief from the itch, each 'patient' was supplied with a bottle containing about half a litre of a white lotion that we were advised to apply to our bodies as and when required. The sight of approximately 50 teenagers and adolescents, clothed in nothing but slips, each smeared white from head to toe was a real spectacle to behold!

Three times a day, the kitchen staff deposited the trolley containing our meals at the door to the isolation unit and rang a bell to alert us that our meals were ready for collection. We opened the door, pulled the trolley inside and served it among ourselves. After we had enjoyed our meals, we deposited the empty plates back in the trolley and pulled it back to the entrance to the isolation unit for it to be collected.

We had no shower in the isolation room. Even if we had, I doubt if anyone would have thought of using it for fear of aggravating the itchy sensation.

After about three weeks of causing menace to our health and disrupting school life, the virus finally bade us a gradual farewell.

-37-
Zero tolerance for agents of addiction!

❖

S moking of cigarettes was strictly forbidden; the same applied to
alcohol; whoever was caught smoking or drinking alcohol risked
suspension or total expulsion from the boarding house. Needless to say
the same thing applied to the use of illicit substances such as cannabis
(Indian hemp), heroin, and cocaine.

I do not claim to be in a position to read the minds of every single
student; from my own observation, however, I can safely say that, at
least as far as my close friends and the majority of the students in my
year group were concerned, the strict rules forbidding participation in
all these activities and substances was not an issue at all. Though rumour
had it that some students, especially some in the senior classes, smoked,
it remained an unsubstantiated rumour.

-38-
Equal rights for women, yes or no?!

I n our boarding school students could join one or more of the few clubs and societies on the campus. Prominent among them were the Dramatic Society, the Debating Society, the Scripture Union and the Cultural Society.

For most part of my time at Odasco, I was a member of both the Dramatic and Debating Societies. I joined both societies quite early during my time at Odasco.

On a few occasions, I took part in some of the plays enacted by the Dramatic Society to entertain the whole school. I was also directly involved in some of the debating sessions organised by the Debating Society for the whole school.

The climax of my engagement with the Debating Society came in May 1976 when, on the occasion of the International Women's Day, I took part in a debate on the theme: *Equal Rights for women, yes or no?*

The audience was not comprised of students of Odasco but rather consisted of a selected group of journalists and dignitaries who met at a location in Akim Oda to mark the occasion.

I was given the difficult role of defending the status quo. Constance, my classmate, vehemently defended the need for society to respect the rights of women.

In the end Constance was declared the winner. To be fair to her, she performed brilliantly. In my opinion, though, she won not because she did better than me, but because she had the bonus of public opinion on her side. Ghanaian society had come a long way since the government of the newly independent country introduced free and compulsory education for every child irrespective of sex and social background in the early sixties. A considerable number of women had already risen to high positions in Ghana.

Much as I tried, I had great difficulty convincing the panel to, as it were, turn the clock of time backwards to the time when women in society were deprived of several opportunities and rights on account of their sex.

Initially, I thought it was a local event. I was therefore pleasantly surprised when I went to the school library to read the newspapers, to find coverage of the event in the *Daily Graphic*, one of the two leading national dailies of the time. Though neither of the two speakers were mentioned by name, the fact that the event had received nationwide coverage gave me great satisfaction.

-39-
The Scripture Unionists

❖

In September 1978, not long after passing out of Sixth Form, I had what Christians refer to as a 'born again' encounter. From then on I made a decision to follow Christ. Prior to that, though I could not be considered an atheist – since I believed in God and ascribed to Christianity – I was not a committed Christian.

As I mentioned earlier, we had to attend Sunday church service – that was also the case when I later moved to Mfantsipim. Nevertheless, I could not at that time be regarded as a dedicated Christian. The suffering in the world in the presence of a loving God tested my faith and brought me to the edge of scepticism.

The situation seemed different for members of the Scripture Union, at least as regards their attitude to the Bible. Apart from the normal Sunday church service, they met on several occasions during their free times for Bible study and fellowship. They shunned opportunities to associate with the rest of us. Even if they attended Saturday evening entertainments, hardly any of them would engage in dancing when it came to disco night. They seemed indeed to be a secluded group.

If the rest of us felt excluded, was it because of envy on our side for their lifestyle? I cannot say for sure. The fact is that members of the SU were generally derided by non-members, who called them all sorts of names. Curiously, members of the group seemed to go about in mixed pairs. Usually the female counterpart would describe the other as a brother in Christ, whereas the male counterpart would speak of his sister in Christ! Though unfounded, rumours made their rounds among the student community that there was something more than met the eye regarding their brother–sister relationship.

-40-
'Operation Feed Yourself'

❖

In the early hours of 13 January 1972, a few days before the beginning of my second term at Odasco, the few residents of Mpintimpi, my father included since he possessed a transistor radio, turned their radios on to be met not with the familiar voices of the regular radio presenters, but with the sound of martial or military music.

'What was the matter?' they wondered.

They did not have to wonder for long, for soon the voice of one Colonel Acheampong interrupted the music.

'Good morning, fellow citizens', he began. 'I am here to announce the overthrow of the Progress Party Regime led by the Prime Minister Dr K.A. Busia. A new junta made up of leading armed forces and police officers, the National Redemption Council, NRC, has taken over the reins of government with immediate effect. Please keep tuned in to radio and television for further announcements!'

'Not again!' was father's first reaction to the news.

The democratically elected government of Dr Busia had been in power for barely 27 months, having taken over from the National Liberation Council (NLC), another military regime, on 1 October 1969. The NLC on its part had overthrown the first post-independence regime of Dr Nkrumah's Convention People's Party (CPP) on 24 February 1966.

The overthrow of the civilian government came as a surprise to many in the village. What however could the ordinary peasants of a settlement such as ours do to influence the course of events at the seat of government in Accra?

101

Not long after assuming the reins of government, the NRC launched the 'Operation Feed Yourself' campaign. As the name implies, the goal of the initiative was to make Ghana self-sufficient in food production. In line with the stated goal, every citizen who was physically able to do so and had a piece of land to serve the purpose was encouraged to grow their own food.

As far as the residents of our little settlement were concerned (and this could be said generally of the peasant population of the countryside) we did not need anyone from the seat of government in Accra, the capital, to lecture us on such matters, *for growing what we eat and eating what we grow* was what we had been practising all along.

This was not the case regarding city or urban dwellers. Prior to the launching of the campaign, backyard gardening was not popular with that group of people. Soon, however, the majority of them were engaged in backyard gardening with the goal of growing basic foodstuffs such as maize, cassava and plantain, as well as vegetables such as tomatoes, garden eggs, carrots, etc., *to feed themselves*.

In the spirit of 'Operation Feed Yourself', boarding school students were also encouraged to produce their own food – if not entirely, at least part of what was required to feed them.

Our school, on its conception, was allocated a large piece of land by the district authorities – land far beyond what was required to build a school of its calibre. Consequently a large part of the school land lay idle.

Prior to the initiation of the Operation Feed Yourself campaign, the agricultural science class utilised part of the land for practical lessons.

With the introduction of the Operation Feed Yourself campaign, the school decided to utilise part of the farmland to grow food. Mr Oteng, the head of the Agricultural Science department, spearheaded Odasco's effort to *feed itself*.

Each house was allocated a piece of farmland to cultivate. In the heat of the campaign, after we had our siesta, we headed for the farmland, which was situated about 300 metres away from the male dormitory block. We did this almost every day of the week, apart from the weekend, and worked on the farm. We remained there until shortly before supper.

From the village dweller like me, who had grown up with farming activity, to the city dwellers – yes, even the children of the elite class who had never before stepped onto farmland – every student became actively involved in the national campaign to become self-reliant in food production.

'Operation Feed Yourself' became so popular in Ghana that the slogan eventually became a household word. From little children to the middle-aged right up to the very elderly, *operation feed yourself* was on the lips of almost everyone.

While popular, it could not be called a 'much *ado about nothing'* movement. At the peak of the campaign, Ghana indeed attained self-sufficiency in food production.

Sadly, owing to several factors that are beyond the remit of this book to explore in detail, the momentum of the campaign could not be sustained indefinitely, and this failure led to the campaign's eventual demise.

Today, as I write, Ghana is far removed from the goal of self-sufficiency in food production that Operation Feed Yourself sought to achieve. With huge arable and fertile land at the disposal of the country, one can only wonder why that is the case, indeed, why the country still has to spend vast sums of money importing food to feed its population.

It is high time the country returned to the spirit of 'Operation Feed Yourself' and mobilised its population and resources towards the production of not only an abundance of food, but also food that can be sold at prices affordable to the average earner.

Indeed, self-sufficiency in food production should be the goal of every country, no matter how poor.

-41-
The passing away of my hero

❖

In the previous chapter I made mention of the fact that Dr Nkrumah's CPP government, which had ruled Ghana since the country's independence from the British on 6 March 1957, was overthrown by the NLC military junta on 24 February 1966.

Following his overthrow, Dr Nkrumah went into exile in Conakry, Guinea. As far as I was concerned, not much was heard about him until 27 April 1972. On that day I returned to the dormitory from lessons to be met with the rumour that Dr Nkrumah had passed away.

Soon the rumour was confirmed by the highest authority in the country. Indeed, not long after hearing about it, Colonel Acheampong, the military head of state at that time, appeared live on radio and TV to announce the passing away of Ghana's first president. Colonel Acheampong went on to state that the sad event had occurred on that very day in a hospital in Bucharest, the Romanian capital, where he had, for a while, been undergoing treatment for an undisclosed ailment.

The life journey of the firebrand pan-African had thus come to an end. On the day of his overthrow six years earlier, I was a Primary Four pupil of Nyafoman Catholic Primary School. One of our peers broke the news to us as we walked in a group from Mpintimpi to attend the school at Nyafoman, a comparatively large village situated two miles to the north of our little village.

I was a boy of about ten at that time. Like my peers on our way to school, the name 'Nkrumah' occupied a high register in my psyche. Though not directly a member of the Young Pioneers, the youth movement of the CPP, like every pupil I had been brought up to hold Ghana, our Motherland, as well as President Nkrumah in very high esteem. Slogans like the following were even on the lips of children of my age:

'I promise on my honour to be faithful and loyal to Ghana my motherland!'

'Forwards ever, backwards never!'

'Africa must unite!'

The news of Nkrumah's overthrow unsettled not only my young brain, but all of us in the group on our way to school. The classmate who broke the news to us went to the extent of telling the group that he had been told that with the overthrow of Nkrumah, the world was going to end! Young as I was, I was scared to the bones on hearing that!

Judging from the reaction of the adult population, the majority of the populace welcomed his overthrow. Indeed, demonstrations in support of his overthrow had taken place throughout the country. The display of support for the coup makers had continued for several weeks.

Even in death, he remained a polarising personality. This was evident from the reaction of the students to the news of his passing away. When I reached the dormitory, I met a group of students who were engaged in a fierce argument that centred on our late former leader. Whereas those who were not inclined towards him took him for a dictator who did not tolerate any form of opposition, his 'fans' defended his record, drawing attention to the numerous developmental projects he undertook during his reign.

I could sense from the heated debates and arguments that raged on for most of the evening that, like me, the majority of the speakers held a favourable opinion of him. Six years on, the tide of public opinion seemed to be turning towards him.

The coup that overthrew him took place at a time when he was out of the country. As might be expected, he was barred from returning to the country. Eventually he was granted political asylum by Guinea. I wondered even then what would happen to his mortal remains after his death. I did not have to wonder for long, for in the course of his broadcast, Colonel Acheampong announced plans not only to return his body to Ghana but also to accord him a state burial.

Initially, his mortal remains were laid to rest at Nkroful, his birthplace. However, in recognition of his role in Ghana and Africa in general, the body was removed to Accra and reburied at the Kwame Nkrumah mausoleum built several years after his death in his honour.

No matter what historians make of his rule, I am personally eternally grateful to him for his free education policy, which enabled me to attend school. Those who do not sympathise with his policies might argue that it was not his personal money that he invested in the several infrastructural projects carried out by his government, including the construction of several schools – primary, secondary as well as institutions of higher learning.

My reply to such individuals is that, unlike many a corrupt African leader, he spent the money for the common good of the population and not for his personal benefit. Indeed, up to now, no one, not even his avowed enemies, have been able to come up with credible evidence to point to personal enrichment on his part during his reign.

Indeed, if other African leaders would emulate his sterling example of selflessness and use national money to build schools, roads, factories and other infrastructural projects, instead of looting state money to deposit it in offshore accounts, the misery plaguing the continent would be reduced, if not completely eliminated.

It is not for nought that in 2000 a BBC ballot nominated Nkrumah as Africa's man of the millennium.

-42-
The tragedy that still lingers in my memory

❖

O ne day, as I was returning to Odasco from Accra where I had spent the mid-term holidays with my brother Ransford, we came to a small town about 20 kilometres from Oda. We had almost driven past the little settlement when, all of a sudden, I heard a loud 'bang'. The loud noise was accompanied by a considerable shaking of the Nissan minibus we were travelling in.

The vehicle had a front cabin separated from the main compartment. The front cabin provided space for the driver and two passengers. The main compartment was made up of two long rows of cushioned seats on either side, each providing space for six passengers. The seating arrangement was such that the passengers sat facing each other with a space of about a metre between them.

I sat on the row nearest the side of the road where the loud noise came from. With my back towards that side of the road, I was unable to witness the events that took place that led to the loud 'bang' just referred to. Not so the driver and some of the passengers who were facing that side of the road.

'My God, he must be dead!' one of the passengers screamed at the top of her voice on hearing the noise.

'My goodness! That poor boy must be crushed to pieces!' another passenger cried in anguish.

Soon the driver brought the vehicle to a stop. All eyes in the vehicle were turned in the direction the noise had come from. Soon it became clear to me what was going on, for I saw lying, at a distance of about 50 metres from our vehicle, the motionless body of what turned out to be a young boy. My heart began to race within me!

The driver, his mate and a few other passengers alighted from the vehicle and rushed to the aid of the poor boy. Soon they carried the victim, a boy whose age I put at around ten, to the vehicle and placed him on the hard floor of the vehicle, in the space between the two rows of seats.

He was clothed with a boy's slip, leaving his top bare. He was not only unconscious, but not breathing. Remarkably, he bore no visible injuries, no cuts, no grazes, no bruises and, as far as I could determine from where I sat, no obvious fractures.

As we learnt later from his parents, he had been playing with his football in the compound of their home not far from the road. Moments before our vehicle reached the area, the ball had strayed to the other side of the road. In his attempt to retrieve it he had ventured onto the road paying, as it turned out, no attention to oncoming traffic.

The nearest hospital was at Akim Oda, my destination, and that of the vehicle. We needed to drive almost half an hour to get there. As we drove on, I could hardly remove my eyes from the lifeless body of the accident victim. Even as I write, the staring gaze of his fixed eyes towards the roof of the vehicle is still fresh in my memory.

We passed a few towns that served as the final destination of some of the travellers before reaching Akim Oda. In view of the emergency situation, however, the driver sped on without stopping until we reached the hospital. Sadly his effort was in vain, for the doctors could only pronounce the injured boy dead on arrival.

Over the next several days, the sight of the motionless body of the accident victim continued to haunt me.

Looking back today, in particular in view of my profession in the medical field, I begin to ask myself: what would have happened had anyone of us made an attempt at resuscitation?

Did any of the passengers have any idea of CPR – cardio pulmonary resuscitation? (CPR is the practice whereby an attempt is made through chest compression and rescue breaths to keep blood and oxygen circulating in the body of a person whose heart has stopped beating and is not breathing.) Speaking for myself, the answer was an emphatic 'NO!' Judging from the faces of the other passengers – their faces indeed portrayed a sense of helplessness in the situation – I can only conclude that hardly anyone of us had ever heard of the concept.

So all of us sat down, passively witnessing the tragedy unfolding before our eyes, without any attempt at active intervention.

Though at that time I had already made up my mind to study medicine, the tragedy, no doubt, helped to strengthen my resolve.

-43-
A flower cruelly snatched from my grip

❖

J ust about the time I was admitted to Oda Secondary School, Ofosu, my most senior brother, the first child of our parents, decided to relocate his tailor's shop from Mpintimpi to Amantia, my mother's hometown, which is about 50 kilometres to the south of Mpintimpi.

During my second year at Odasco, after spending most of my holidays at Mpintimpi, I decided to visit Amantia to spend the last remaining few days of the holidays with my senior brother.

Adwoa, my sister who comes immediately behind me on the family tree, also happened to be visiting Amantia at the same time. Three days before the end of the holidays she left home to play with her friends. On her return home, she was accompanied by one of her friends, a girl of about her age.

You may call it love at first sight between me and her, if you will! In any event we soon developed a deep affection for each other. Even before we could find time to further develop our friendship, however, the boarding school chap had to return to school! Fortunately, my new-found friend had a photograph, something that was not common in our setting at that time. So, as a parting gift, she gave me a photo of herself.

When I got back to Oda, I told my close friends, George and Emmanuel, about the latest development in my life. Perhaps I bored them with my constant reference to 'the flower of my life'. I am sure I did. Probably out of respect for their friend in the burning flush of love, they put up with me and refrained from pointing out that I was getting on their nerves with my constant reference to Akosua, my new friend!

Indeed, her picture became my closet 'companion'. At that time there were no telephone links between Oda and the village. The only form of communication was by means of letter. It was perhaps not surprising, therefore, that I wrote a great many letters to my new friend.

At long last what I had yearned for, the school vacation, arrived. I could not head straight to Amantia, however. Instead I had to travel first to Mpintimpi.

As on the previous occasion, I managed to persuade my parents to permit me to spend the few remaining days of the vacation with my senior bother at Amantia. I would then continue on to Odasco without the need to return to Mpintimpi. Even as I spent the holidays at Mpintimpi, I was impatient for the days to fly by! At long last, the long awaited day came for me to leave Mpintimpi for Amantia.

As I bade farewell to my parents, my mother, who apparently had received a tip-off from my sister Adwoa regarding the friendship that was developing between me and her friend Akos (short for Akosua), turned to me and said:

'Are you sure you are going to Amantia just because of Ofosu? '

'Sure!' I lied.

'Sure?' she asked in a voice that betrayed her suspicion.

'Sure, sure!'

'On your honour?'

'Yes, yes! What else do you think I am going there for?'

'Well', she said knowingly, 'as the Twi saying goes, "The death of an animal may go unnoticed – until it decomposes to fill the air with the stench!"'

'You and your sophisticated proverbs!' I replied.

'Well, let's wait and see!'

One can imagine my joy when I finally stepped on the soil of Amantia. I arrived late in the evening so I decided to rest before attempting to venture outside. Owing to the reasons familiar to the reader, Akosua was unaware of my coming.

The next evening I ventured into the central area of the town, to a spot that served as the main point of interaction for the community, especially the youth, at night. It was a moonlit night, a fact that helped to draw many out of their homes.

About half an hour after my arrival at the 'community centre' I finally spotted 'the flower of my life!' I hurried towards her! But instead of the warm greeting – a warm embrace and probably a kiss on the cheek – that I expected, to my utter surprise she turned and walked away on seeing me, leaving me, literally, frozen to the spot! I was flabbergasted, indeed, shocked to the core!

After the initial surprise, I decided to make a second attempt. Perhaps she had taken me for a stranger and failed to recognise me, I reasoned. She had in the meantime taken her place at a spot about 20 metres from where I stood. I headed in that direction. As I drew closer, I began:

'Look here, Akos, it is *me*, your friend! I am now on vacation.'

'And so what?' she retorted and walked quickly away, heading in the direction of her home which was about a hundred metres away.

I was so stunned, for a moment, that I thought I was in a bad dream instead of the real world! Still not able to fathom what was unfolding before my eyes, I left for home. Could I sleep through the night? Well somehow I did, but not soundly, I must confess. For much of the night I just wondered what had led to her strange behaviour. Was it possible that someone had told her a tall story that I had found another friend at the boarding house? Or had she herself found someone else?

The next day, what I had suspected was confirmed before my very eyes. As I sat at in my brother's workshop, which happened to be on the main street of the little town, I spotted her, walking by the side of a gentleman who happened to be several years her senior. My heart began to race within me; my whole body began to shiver violently.

Was this a way of intentionally imparting even more pain to my already broken heart? I did not know for sure. In any case, just as they walked past me, he grasped her firmly with his arm and drew her closely to his side! I just could not bear the scene any longer. Excusing myself from my brother I left and headed home, never to return to the street that day.

If I had my own way, I would have left Amantia the very next day – but I had no choice but to hang on and spend the few remaining days of the holidays there. I had taken all my belongings with me when I left

Mpintimpi for Amantia. Father would have been furious with me for the additional financial burden he would need to shoulder if I returned to Mpintimpi to await the end of the vacation.

In the course of time, I got to know some details about my rival. He happened to be the purchasing clerk of the Cocoa Marketing Board in the village. It was no secret that such clerks were well-to-do in the communities where they were stationed. Rumours made their rounds that it was their custom to cheat the mainly illiterate farmers who came there to sell their produce. In any case he had taken advantage of his heavy purse as well as my absence to, as it were, pluck my rose from me!

As might be expected, on my return to Odasco I was silent on the matter. Not for long, though. A few days after our return to school, George, my closest friend, turned to me and began:

'How is Akosua?'

'Which Akosua?'

'Friend, you should know!'

'Well, she has gone her own way!'

'I don't believe it! What happened?'

At that stage I saw no other alternative than to let the cat out of the bag.

Several years have elapsed since then. Her friendship with the clerk lasted only a few months as it happened. Several years later she went on to marry someone else.

We have remained good friends to this day. Whenever I visit Amantia, if she happens to be in town, she comes round to say hello. On such occasions we would reminisce over our youthful friendship that was torn asunder even before it could take root!

-44-

The trusted black and white TV and the Rumble in the Jungle

❖

During my time at Odasco there was a single black and white TV set for the whole male population. The same thing applied to our female counterparts. The male TV set rarely displayed good clear pictures. That did not prevent those keen on watching a particular programme from doing so!

The male TV was locked up in a cupboard in a room adjacent to the dining hall. The keys to the room and also the cupboard that contained it were entrusted to the entertainment prefect. When he was prevented from doing so himself, he delegated the responsibility of unlocking the TV room to a trusted senior student.

At the time in question the only channel available to viewers nationwide was GBC TV, the state-owned broadcasting corporation. Not only did the whole population have access to only a single TV channel, the only provider did not operate around the clock. Instead, GBC-TV came on air around 5 p.m. and went off air around midnight each day.

We were permitted to watch TV only during the weekends. Though in theory every student could watch it, Form One and Two students generally stayed away from it – in their own interests, I should add. It is not surprising that there was usually not much space in the TV room to accommodate everyone desirous of watching a programme. Based on what I mentioned earlier in regard to the practice of *homoing*, a junior student who dared compete with a senior student for the limited space could be made to face the music for what amounted in the eyes of the senior to a show of insolence! Personally, it was when I got to Form Three that I dared venture to go to the TV room.

The TV programme that was most popular as far as the male students were concerned was the live transmission of the national football league matches on Sunday afternoons. Though league matches were played in various locations in the country, at that time GBC-TV was technically capable of broadcasting LIVE coverage from only the Accra sports stadium. The two leading teams in Ghana then were Accra Hearts of Oak and Kumasi Asante Kotoko. As their names suggest, the two clubs had their homes in Accra, the capital, and Kumasi the second largest city respectively.

George, my best friend at Odasco, and I were supporters of Kumasi Asante Kotoko – not ordinary fans but real ardent supporters. We could indeed be counted among the type of fans who completely lose their appetite and their ability to sleep well when their favourite teams lose a game. Indeed, whenever 'Fabu, Fabu' (short for Fabulous Asante Kotoko) lost a game, for a while my world seemed to have come to an end.

Emmanuel Awatey and Kofi Anning, my other close mates, were passionate supporters of Accra Hearts of Oak.

Whenever 'Fabu, Fabu' met Accra Hearts of Oak at the Accra Sports stadium, there was real tension in the air, not only among friends supporting the opposing side, but among avid supporters of each club in general. Whoever wanted to watch the event on TV had to appear there several minutes before the keyholder could get there, to ensure securing even a standing position.

Another show that drew considerable viewership, not only at Odasco but nationwide, was Osofo Dadzie – a soap opera that dealt in the main with burning social issues of the day. The 30-minute show ran from 8:30 to 9:00 p.m. on Sundays. Those wishing to watch it moved straight from the Sunday evening service to the TV room.

'Talking Point', a current affairs programme that aired just before the Osofo Dadzie show, was also popular, not only for me but a good deal of the students.

It would be a disservice to our beloved black and white TV if I ended this chapter without saying something about a spectacular sporting event of international dimensions that it helped bring to our doorsteps.

I am referring here to the global boxing event that to this day is well remembered by many as the *Rumble in the Jungle* – the historic heavyweight fight between the then champion George Foreman and his challenger Mohammed Ali, which took place on 30 October 1974 at the May 20 Stadium in Kinshasa, the Democratic Republic of the Congo, then Zaire.

I was then in Form Four. Owing to the huge popularity it had gained among the student population, the authorities for once permitted us not only to place the TV in the large dining hall but also to stay awake past the time we were usually expected to be in our various beds.

Mohammed Ali won the epic duel through a knock-out in the eighth round. For reasons that I cannot exactly recall, the majority of us supported the challenger. Though hardly any of his ardent supporters reckoned with a win against the younger and more energetic Foreman, as it turned out that is exactly what happened.

For several minutes after the fight, the chants of 'Ali you are the greatest! Ali you are the greatest! Ali you are the greatest!!!' filled the night air of the school premises.

-45-
The youth molester and the hopeless Ghanaian

◈

At the beginning of one long vacation, which usually lasted from the end of June to the middle of September, I left for a visit to Ransford in Accra after spending a few days at Mpintimpi. At the back of my mind was the desire to find a vacation employment that would enable me to earn some money for the next academic year.

At that time Ransford was a resident of Asylum Down, a suburb of Accra. Also living in the same apartment block was Moses, popularly known by us by his alias Papiito, a not too distant relation of mine. Not only were we related, we used to be classmates at elementary school. He was a brilliant pupil and may well have made it to secondary school, if only he had had someone to finance his education. Without the necessary financial support, he had to content himself with a middle school leaving certificate.

After completing his elementary education he moved to Accra in search of work. Eventually he found employment as part of the kitchen staff at a Lebanese restaurant, about half a kilometre from where he lived.

When I arrived in Accra in search of a vacation job, he offered to speak to his boss on my behalf.

'No problem', his boss told him, 'we can take him on as a dishwasher. He can start tomorrow if he likes.'

I was delighted at the opportunity to earn some pocket money. The next day I accompanied him to work. Soon I was busily engaged as dishwasher in the kitchen of the Lebanese restaurant which happened to be situated in Adabraka, a suburb of Accra bordering on Asylum Down.

I enjoyed my work, not only because of the opportunity to earn some money for school, but it gave me access to free meals whenever I was on duty. However, about three weeks into what would have been an eight-week job, my engagement came to an abrupt end!

One day, as I went about my duty, with the usual diligence I might add, for reasons that I can no longer recall, I lost hold of a ceramic plate I was in the process of cleaning. 'Bang!' it went, crashing onto the floor, breaking into several pieces! I reported the matter to the team leader, who in turn informed the owner. Soon the owner appeared from his office, anger written all over his face.

'What happened?' he inquired in a stern voice.

Even before I could reply, his outstretched hand was heading towards my face. The slap on my face was so unexpected that I had no time to dodge it! 'Wham!' – it landed on the side of my face nearest to him. It came with such force that I struggled to keep my balance.

'Tell me what happened!' the irate owner demanded.

He attempted to slap me a second time. On this occasion I managed to duck!

The blood meanwhile began to boil in my head! My instant reaction was to act in line with 'an eye for an eye' and hit back. Very quickly it dawned on me that I would probably not be a match for him; so instead of doing anything to escalate the situation, I decided to put some distance between myself and my attacker. I escaped through the main entrance and took my position on the pavement adjacent to the busy street. There I began to ponder my next move.

'How in heaven's name could that foreigner treat me in that manner in my own country?' I mused. 'Why indeed should that happen to me in Kwame Nkrumah's Ghana?' I asked myself

As I mentioned earlier, during my primary school days, though I was not a member of the Young Pioneers, we had been taught patriotism and been introduced to the concept of the African personality, which emphasised the fact that Africans were equal among others of other race and colour.

As far us our country Ghana was concerned, we were taught to look upon ourselves as masters in our 'Land of birth', our motherland, as we termed it.

Foreigners were welcome to live with us; certainly, they were welcome to taste the traditional Ghanaian hospitality – but they should nevertheless respect our rightful roles as first class citizens of our country.

At that juncture, one of the independent slogans of Nkrumah came to mind: 'We prefer self-government in danger to servitude in tranquillity.' I said to myself: 'I would never, for the sake of money, allow myself to be humiliated in my own country. No, never!'

At that very moment, I resolved that that day was going to be the last day I would work for the youth molester! Gathering courage, I re-entered the premises and headed straight to the staff locker where we kept our personal items. Without informing anyone of my intention, I opened it and pulled out my belongings.

'What are you doing?' one of my colleagues inquired.

'Quitting the job!'

'But you need the money!'

'To hell with his money!' I replied, 'I won't allow a foreigner to humiliate me in my own country. He may choose to maltreat me in Beirut, but not in Accra!'

As I headed home, it occurred to me that I should not allow the matter to rest there; instead, I would ask my brother Ransford to go and teach him a lesson in good behavior.

Ghana at that time was still being ruled by Colonel Acheampong and the NLC. The military was feared by the populace.

Who dared have a case with a soldier in those days? Even if it was not sanctioned from above, the military could take the law into their own hands and teach one a lesson in good behaviour – whatever their definition of good behaviour was! It was indeed a period in our history when it was 'something' to be a soldier! Though Ransford, then a junior officer in the Air Force, could not be counted among the 'Rambos' of his 'race', confronting the offending foreigner in his uniform could send a cold chill down the offender's spine.

As might be expected, Ransford was furious on hearing what I had to tell him. Though he happened to be off duty, he hurriedly put on his uniform and accompanied me to the restaurant.

The offender was clearly taken aback on seeing us. After Ransford informed him of the reason for our coming, he demanded to know his side of the story. I thought he would tell the truth and apologise for his deed. But no! Instead, he denied categorically the charge levelled against him.

'That's a lie!' I replied in rage.

'Who is lying, my friend?' he countered.

At that stage Ransford turned to me and inquired: 'Did anyone witness it?'

'Yes, of course, I have a witness.'

'Who?'

'Our team leader!'

'Sure?'

'Yes. He hit me in the presence of the team leader.'

At that stage the manager turned to one of the workers nearby: 'Go fetch your team leader', he said, beckoning to the worker.

Soon our team leader, a man in his mid-40s, emerged from one area of the restaurant.

'What is the matter?' he inquired nervously as he approached us.

'This guy is accusing me of slapping him. According to him you witnessed the incident. Now, tell his brother, did I do anything to him?'

'No, sir!' the team leader replied without a moment's hesitation!

Hardly able to believe my ears, I looked at him in bewilderment.

'You're a liar!' I screamed at him.

'But I can see hand marks on his face,' Ransford remarked, pointing to the fresh fingermarks on my left cheek.

'Well, you wanted to know from me whether I witnessed the incident. I have given you my answer. That is all that I can say in the matter.'

'You are afraid to tell the truth!' I screamed at him. 'A hopeless Ghanaian you are indeed!'

'Who is a hopeless Ghanaian?'

'You!' I shouted at the top of my voice.

Without any witness to back me up, the confrontation turned out to be *a claim and counter-claim affair*.

In the end Ransford advised me that we should leave the matter as it was and not pursue it any further. Neither was it our intention to pursue the case in court. We just wanted the manager to admit his fault and eventually apologise for what he had done. I regarded him a coward, one who was afraid to stand up to his own actions.

I felt very let down by my fellow countryman. He lacked the courage to confront the offender for fear of retribution. He seemed certainly more interested in keeping his job than bearing testimony to what he had witnessed!

-46-
The gamble that paid off

❖

A t the beginning of Form Five I began preparations not only for the GCE 'O'-Level examinations but also for the time thereafter. In regard to the immediate post-GCE 'O'-Level period, each student faced three prospects, which in general depended on the grades obtained at the GCE 'O'-Levels.

The first prospect, which almost everyone yearned for, was to obtain the necessary grades to ensure admission to Sixth Form.

Those who did quite well, but not well enough to gain admission to Sixth Form, could be admitted to teacher training schools to do a two-year post-secondary education course to qualify as elementary school teachers.

Those whose grades were too low to enable them to pursue any of the paths outlined above, could choose to do remedial courses with a view to improving their results, finding employment or both.

Several weeks before we took our examinations, those wishing to be considered for admission to Sixth Form and/or post-secondary education needed to complete the necessary forms.

Not every secondary school offered Sixth Form education. 'O'-Level leavers from such schools had no choice but to look beyond the boundary of their schools for suitable schools to apply to. I did not face that problem since Oda Secondary School was a Sixth Form school. Still, I looked beyond the boundaries of Oda Secondary for my Sixth Form education.I selected Mfantsipim School as my first choice and

Oda as my second – to the disappointment of my teachers who wanted to keep one of their bright students.

It was a bold decision and not made without risk. The school naturally would give preference to its own 'O'-Level candidates desirous of completing their further education there. Since it had become an elite school I expected to face, in addition, competition from the children of the rich and mighty of society who desired to move there from elsewhere for the Sixth Form course. This meant the only way I could 'make it' there was to distinguish myself in the 'O'-Level examination.

Overflowing with self-confidence, I sought in my own small way to make a political statement, to the effect that the children of peasant farmers such as Kofi Gyamfi and Amma Owusuah of little Mpintimpi, given the chance, were capable of competing in the same league as the children of the affluent and powerful.

And so it transpired! Emerging as the best student of my year group at Oda Secondary School – the only candidate to pass out with Grade 1 distinction – Mfantsipim opened its doors to me in the academic year 1976–1977.

-47-
Happy birthday proud centenarian

❖

In October 1976 I began my two-year Sixth Form course at Mfantsipim Secondary School. As I mentioned earlier, the school prided itself as being the first secondary school to be built in the country. Situated in Cape Coast, a coastal city located about 100 kilometres to the west of the capital Accra, it was built by the Methodist Missionaries to the then Gold Coast.

1976, the year of my admission, was a special year as far as the school was concerned. Readers will recall that I mentioned earlier on that the school was founded in 1876 – so 1976 was its first centenary year. Throughout the year, special events were organised to mark the anniversary. The celebrations were climaxed by a huge and colourful centenary day event held in September of that year.

Since the results of the GCE 'O'-Level examination were released in August/September, and also because the selection process for Lower Sixth Formers took some time to complete, Lower Sixth Formers were usually admitted in October – too late for those admitted in the centenary year to be part of the climax event.

We did not go empty-handed, however. To mark the anniversary, a special anniversary *ntama* – a Ghanaian traditional cloth worn by wrapping it around the body – had been released. Each student, including Lower Sixth Formers who had missed the main event, was required to acquire the piece.

-48-
Comparing and contrasting alma maters

❖

Mfantsipim was different from Odasco in several respects.
First there is the topography. Whereas Odasco was spread over an almost flat and even landscape, Mfatsipim School was built on the Kwabotwe Hill.

Odasco was situated about five kilometres away from Akim Oda, the town bearing its name. There was nothing apart from farmland separating the two. Mfantsipim, in earlier times, was some distance away from the city centre. In time the city expanded towards it. Presently the city borders stretch, literally, to the main gate of the school.

Whereas Odasco was a mixed school, Mfantsipim, at least in our time, admitted only boys. Was it because of the absence of the opposite sex to serve as a distraction? Although I was used to serious academic work at Oda, I was astonished to realise the zeal with which Kwabotwe (in alluding to the name of the hill on which it is located, Mfatsipim is also affectionately referred to as Kwabotwe, especially among the student population) boys went about their studies. From Form One students, right up to Upper Sixth Form students, everyone seemed to be occupied with nothing but their books.

Mfantsipim could without doubt be described as an elite school. Being the first secondary school of the country, a considerable number of famous personalities had passed through its gates by the time I was admitted there. Alumni of the school include Kofi Annan, Nobel Prize winner and former Secretary-General of the United Nations; Dr Kofi

Abrefa Busia, Ghana's prime minister from 1969 to 1972 and Joseph W.S. de Graft-Johnson, Vice President of Ghana from 1979 to 1981.

Not only did Mfantsipim boast famous past students, it was highly regarded by the rich and powerful of society in their search for a suitable secondary school for their children. During my time there, one of the children of Colonel Acheampong, the military head of state, was a student there.

In contrast, Odasco was a young school that needed time to establish its status in society

Another feature of Mfantsipim that struck me was the relatively young age of the student population as compared to those of Oda. The average age of Form One students was around 12 years.

In contrast I was a month shy of my 16th birthday at the time I was admitted to Form One at Odasco; that may well have been the average age of most of my Form One classmates.

The age difference between students of the two schools might be explained on the basis of what I mentioned at the beginning of my narration concerning the state elementary schools and the privately run preparatory schools. The well-to-do sent their children to such schools at the early age of five or six years, leading them to attempt the common entrance examination at the age of 11 or 12 years.

Oda Secondary School, at least from my perspective, had one important advantage over Mfantsipim. The food served at Mfantsipim, while being of good quality, rarely matched that offered at Oda in quantity. As I mentioned earlier, at Oda, particularly during the weekends, many female students stayed away from the dining hall – to the delight of the male students. That the quantity of food served at Cape Coast was not sufficient to satisfy the average student was no secret. This did not bother the majority of students, however. Needless to say, most of them had the means at their disposal to supplement the meals served. For reasons already known to the reader, this could not be said of yours truly.

There was an unpleasant way in which Mfantsipim differed from Odasco. Odasco was isolated, surrounded only by vegetation. The school, which has been built from scratch, was barely ten years old at the time of my admission. The surroundings were quite neat. It also boasted a good canalisation system.

Mfantsipim on the other hand was almost encircled by the city. Although the school compound was neat and well kept, that could not be said of the city itself. The canalisation of the city was not only exposed at many points, it was also filled in many places with filth. Apart from that, there were in several parts of the city standing ponds filled with dirty water, with filthy surroundings. These areas served as breeding grounds for mosquitoes. In the evening, hordes of them left their breeding grounds and flew towards the Mfantsipim school compound in search of their 'dinner'.

Although sleeping under mosquito nets was recommended at Odasco, hardly anyone found the need to do so; at Mfantsipim, hardly any of us dared to go to sleep without them.

Of course there were some similarities between the two schools. In those days both schools admitted only boarders. Both were publicly financed second-cycle schools, offering second-cycle education up till Sixth Form.

-49-

Akim Oda Diamonds versus Cape Coast Castles

In as much as there were differences and similarities between Odasco and Mfantsipim, there were differences between Akim Oda and Cape Coast – their respective locations.

Akim Oda is a district capital, with more rural surroundings. Traditionally, it is the seat of the Omanhene of the Akim Kotoku traditional area. For the sake of those unfamiliar with matters relating to chieftaincy in Ghana, the Omanhene or paramount chief of a traditional area has several smaller chiefs under him.

Commercial activity in Akim Oda centres mainly on agriculture as well as small-scale diamond mining along the banks of the Birim river about a kilometre to its northern perimeters.

As for matters of historical importance, Akim Oda does not have much to offer.

Cape Coast, also known by its local name Oguaa, was first named Cape Coast – Carbo Corso – by the Portuguese who were the first Europeans to arrive there in the 15th century. On their arrival, the Portuguese set up their base on a small hill overlooking the Atlantic Ocean.

In the course of time the property fell into the hands of the Dutch, who converted it into a castle in 1650.

In 1652, the Swedes took the castle from the Dutch and expanded it further.

In 1664 the British captured the castle from the Swedes and eventually made Cape Coast the capital of the British colonial administration. This was the case until 1877 when it was moved to Accra.

Traditionally it is the seat of the paramount chief of the Oguaa traditional area.

Commercial activity of Cape Coast revolves around fishing and tourism. Indeed, the Cape Coast castle, which served as a transit location for slaves awaiting further shipment to their final destinations in the Americas and elsewhere, has become a tourist attraction.

Not only does Cape Coast have the distinction of being the location of the first and foremost secondary school in Ghana, it has become home to many leading secondary and technical institutions. Apart from Mfantsipim School, it is also the home of the following well-known schools: Wesley Girls, St Augustines, Holy Child School, Adisadel College, Aggrey Memorial Secondary School, Ghana National College and Cape Coast Technical Institute.

It is also home to the University of Cape Coast, one of the leading universities in the country.

It is not for nought that Cape Coast is referred to as the Educational Capital of Ghana. Indeed, nowhere else in the country are so many reputable secondary schools and other institutions of higher learning concentrated within such a small area.

The perpetual rivalry of the Methodist and Anglican boys of two Cape Coast schools

The concentration of schools in the small locality of Cape Coast led to rivalry amongst them. Talking of rivalry between the schools in the area: the extent of rivalry between Mfantsipim School on the one hand and Adisadel College, an Anglican boys' secondary school, on the other, surpasses all others. Indeed, the rivalry between the two reputable schools is known not only within the borders of each school, but extends beyond their respective borders to Cape Coast and beyond.

Whenever the two schools were paired in a sporting event – athletics, football, field hockey, table tennis etc. – tension would build up over several days if not weeks prior to the occasion. When the day finally arrived the tension became almost palpable.

Mfantsipim could afford to lose to other schools in the city and elsewhere – we could live with that; not so in the case of a defeat by Adisadel. Whenever that happened, the world of Mfantsipim seemed to crumble beneath our feet.

The rivalry existed not only in the area of sport; it extended also into the academic realm. Whenever the results of the 'O' and 'A'-Levels for a particular year were released, everyone at Mfantsipim was eager to know not only the overall performance of our school, but also that of our arch rivals. How many Grade 1 distinctions did their 'O'-Level students attain vis-à-vis us? What about their 'A'-Level students? How many of them were able to achieve the ultimate – four As? Did they perform better than us?

A similar degree of rivalry existed between Wesley Girls and Holy Child, the two leading girls' schools in the city.

One does not encounter only rivalry between Cape Coast Schools, but also bonds of friendship. By virtue of both being Methodist schools, there was and there still is a close bond of friendship between Mfantsipim School on the one hand and Wesley Girls' School (also known popularly as Debu Girls) on the other.

Not only do the two schools share a common confession or faith, there is a considerable degree of interpersonal relationships between students of the two schools. Indeed, many a student at Mfantsipim had a relation at Debu – a sister, cousin, aunt, etc.

Even if they were not directly related, a considerable number of students from both schools had attended the same preparatory school prior to their admission to the respective school. The primary school friendship was kept alive at the secondary school level. As a result, a great deal of socialisation took place between students of the two schools.

I must add that the special relationship just described was not unique to Mfantsipim and Wesley Girls. The same could be said of the boys-only Catholic boarding school, St Augustine's Secondary School, on the one hand, and Holy Child School, their female counterpart of the same confession, on the other.

-51-
African tradition on display in Sunday worship service

❖

I n October 1976, I enrolled as a Lower Six student at Mfantsipim
Secondary School. There were two groups of Lower Six students.
The first group consisted of former students who had done their 'O'-
Levels there and were returning for the Sixth Form course.

The second group of students consisted of students like me, who
had completed their 'O'-Levels elsewhere and were at Mfantsipim
Secondary School for the first time.

As might be expected, the first group of students did not encounter
any issues relating to adaptation; not so the second group. Indeed, it
took me some time to adapt to my new environment.

The situation was quite different from the time I arrived at Odasco
for the first time, however. At that time, I was a *greenhorn*, subjected to
homoing. This time I was a *senior boy,* who was accorded due respect
by *junior boys*. Indeed, senior boys, especially those in the Lower and
Upper Six were highly respected, even literally revered, especially by
Form One and Two students.

What junior boy would dare do or say anything untoward to a senior
boy! Well, they could say or express their displeasure or dislike towards
senior boys behind their backs, far away from their ears; but they would
never do so in their hearing, not even in the company of others who
might report them to the senior boy concerned!

I was housed in Sarbah-Picot House. There were five other houses:
Balmer-Acquah, Bartels-Sneath, Freeman-Aggrey, Pickard-Parker,

Lockhart-Schweitzer. As I found out later, most of the houses bore the names of past headmasters of the school.

I found the student population generally disciplined, well-behaved and polite. The need to comport oneself well was not imposed from above – it had become part and parcel of student life. Everyone behaved decently; anyone who behaved contrary to the generally acceptable pattern became conspicuous.

To cite an example – everyone was required to tuck in their shirt instead of allowing it to hang over the trousers. Everyone one met on the premises – whether on the way to attend lessons, whether heading for the dining hall or whether walking leisurely around, was found with the shirt tucked in.

As far as the daily boarding house routine went, it was similar to what I was used to at Odasco – not only during weekdays but also the weekends.

It was in the area of what we wore for Sunday evening worship service that I noticed a difference between the two schools. Readers might recall that in Odasco we dressed in 'white-white' and put on our school tie. Perhaps keen on upholding our African tradition, Mfantsipim prescribed *ntama* as the formal wear for Sunday evening worship service.

-52-
A female role model

❖

A student applying for admission to medical school in Ghana in those days was required to present three above-average GCE A-Level passes in physics, chemistry and biology or mathematics. Desirous of pursuing my dream of studying medicine, I offered biology, physics and chemistry for the Sixth Form.

Both our physics and chemistry teachers were male; not so our biology teacher. Miss Dovlo was a self-confident, energetic and dedicated person who had a great passion for her subject, biology.

In Ghana, generally, parents have not been known to discriminate against their daughters when it comes to the education of their children. Prior to the introduction of free and compulsory education by the first post-independence government, it was affordability that determined whether parents sent their children to school or not.

With the introduction of free education for all, every child of school-going age irrespective of their sex as well as the religious and social backgrounds of their parents were expected to be enrolled in schools. The policy was not only recorded on paper; it was enforced to the letter by the educational authorities. Parents who attempted to prevent their children from going to school faced prosecution. (Some peasant farmers yearning for the days when their children provided helping hands on the farms might otherwise not have complied with the directive.)

Our charismatic, energetic and engaging biology teacher was the epitome of all that stands for female education. She is, no doubt, a sterling example or role model to point to for campaigners for the right of education for girls worldwide.

-53-
My lately discovered little brother

❖

W hen I arrived in Germany, some of my German friends who were familiar with my marital status wondered why I had a compound name. I understood where they were coming from, for in that society double-barrelled names are not common. It is only when married couples decide, against the usual practice where a woman adopts the name of the husband, to form a family name out of the combination of the names of the two involved, that such names arise.

In response to their query, I usually set out to give them a brief lecture on how my name combination came about. I would start by pointing out to them that, as far as the Akan tradition goes, the present form of my name can be considered a colonial legacy. Indeed as far as members of the Akan traditional group in Ghana, of which I am a member, are concerned, prior to their interaction with the Europeans, compound names were unknown.

It was also not customary for an Akan child to adopt the name of the father. The same was true of a married woman; she too did not have to assume the name of her husband.

When an Akan child is eight days old, a naming ceremony is organised during which the name of the child is officially made known to the public. Usually Akan parents name their children after relatives or other personalities of good standing in the community past and present.

In my case, my parents decided to name me after Nana Kofi Peprah, one of father's maternal uncles. It was not for nought that father decided to give that particular uncle that honour. Father indeed might have passed away a few weeks prior to my birth had it not been for the timely intervention of the generous uncle.

As father used to narrate to his children who either were too young to remember or were not born at that time, when mother was heavily pregnant with me, a small boil developed on his left thigh. In time it grew bigger and bigger. For reasons of poverty (they were ordinary peasant farmers who struggled to make ends meet) and lack of knowledge (it was generally held by the local populace that treatment for boils did not belong to the remit of conventional medicine but rather that of traditional healers), no medical help was sought. In time his condition deteriorated to the point that everyone began to reckon with the worst. Even at that point, he was kept at home!

Fortunately, just at that moment in time, Nana Kofi Peprah, who resided in a town about 120 kilometres to the north of Mpintimpi, arrived for a chance visit. He was shocked on seeing the condition of my seriously ill father.

'Why haven't you sent him to hospital?' he inquired in a voice filled with anger and disbelief. Without hesitating a moment he arranged for his seriously ill nephew to be sent to a hospital not far from his place of residence and into the care of a doctor friend of his.

Happily, father survived.

When I finally made it to the planet I had elected to visit, my proud father did not hesitate for a moment in naming me after his magnanimous uncle. Thus I became known as Kofi Peprah; not Kofi Gyamfi as would have been the case had I had to carry my father's name. Even to this day, Kofi Peprah is the name by which I am known in my little village.

Eventually Kofi Peprah became *Koopra!*

'Koopra, behave!' Father would caution his little boy whenever I did something that was naughty in his eyes.

'Koopra, go fetch water for your father!' Mother would instruct her teenage boy to join his peers and walk a distance of about half a mile to the Nwi River and fetch water in a bucket, carry it on his head, and present it to his 'Old Man' so he could have his daily bath.

'Koopra, let's play football', one of my peers would invite me to join him in what was the favourite game of almost every lad in the village.

Koopra here, Koopra there! Thus the village boy with the big 'coconut' head and the protruding belly (a victim of *Kwashiorkor*, caused by lack of protein in my meals) went about his daily activities on the streets of Mpintimpi.

In former times, long, long before the Europeans decided to visit Africa – *for reasons best known to them, I might add* – I would have carried that name to the grave.

With the arrival of Europeans on our shores, things began to change. Children enrolling to attend school for the first time were not only expected to adopt European first names, but also the names of their fathers. (Eventually, married women were also 'called upon' to adopt the names of the husbands.)

In my case, I adopted the European first name Robert when I started school. Initially I was known only as Robert Kofi Peprah. Later, when I was completing the forms to register for the common entrance examination, I was required to fill in the name of my father. I filled in Robert Kofi as my first names and Peprah Gyamfi as my surname.

At Odasco the two names Peprah Gyamfi were usually written together – not with a binding hyphen, though.

I do not know whether it had to do with the manner in which I filled the Sixth Form admission forms. In any case, when I got to Mfantsipim the name Gyamfi nearly *disappeared* from my *set of names*. Instead of the two names Peprah Gyamfi appearing side by side as had been the case at Odasco, my name appeared only as Peprah, R.G. on all official documents.

That fact would eventually lead me to my *'new little brother'* – Alex Peprah! When I arrived at Mfantsipim for my Sixth Form course, Alex was already in Form One, having arrived there a few weeks before me. As I learnt from him, his father was one Mr Peprah, then managing director of the Eastern Region Development Corporation, a quasi-state organisation with its headquarters at Koforidua, the capital of the Eastern Region, about 70 kilometres to the north of Accra.

As far as my memory goes, there were only two 'Peprahs' in the school population of about a thousand students.

I do not exactly remember the circumstances that brought us together – it had something to do with our common name, I suppose.

145

In any case, not long after my arrival at Mfantsipim, I became not only the mentor of Alex, who was a little over 11 years old at that time, but gained the distinction of being his 'big brother'. I do not know whether we did indeed bear some resemblance to each other; but the fact is that in the course of time our classmates did indeed regard us to be siblings. Whenever *little Peprah* was naughty to someone, he was reported to his *big brother.*

Not only did he place his chop box in my care, as his 'big brother'; he also entrusted me with his valuables, including money. Not only that, he was also privileged to spend time in the senior boys' room, a sort of annex attached to each house, providing accommodation to the house prefect and a few other Upper Six students.

Usually Alex's parents arranged for him to be fetched with their private car when school closed for vacations. On the few occasions when that was not the case, we travelled together on the same commuter bus to Accra. On arrival there, I helped him get a connecting bus home before continuing on my journey.

When I left Mfantsipim, contact between my *'little brother'* and I continued for a while, but eventually ended. Was it his fault, or was it mine? Whatever the case, somewhere along the line, communication between us became severed completely. With the advent of the internet I have tried with the help of social media and other means available on the world wide web to re-establish contact, but to no avail – at least until now.

-54-

The tragic passing of a schoolmate

❖

I not only experienced the joy of gaining a brother at Mfantsipim, but also experienced the painful loss of a mate. The tragedy surrounding that parting touched me to the extent that, even as I write, it remains as if freshly engraved in my memory.

As in the case of Odasco, students could, with official permission, leave the premises of the boarding school at the weekend. Usually those who left the school on normal exeats were expected to return the same day. Those wishing to spend the weekend at home needed special permits to do so.

As I mentioned earlier, Cape Coast boasts several schools. Not only that, there are also quite a few boarding schools in its immediate surroundings. Among them is Mfantsiman Girls' School at Saltpond, a large town about 30 kilometres to the east of Cape Coast.

As was usually the case in all boarding schools, each dormitory had a captain selected from the students of the most senior class. His duty was to see to it that order prevailed in the hostel. He selected other students to help him in his duties. The house captain was accountable to the housemaster. Every evening a roll call was conducted by the captain to make sure everyone was present.

One Sunday, towards the end of my second and final year at Mfantsipim, rumours began to circulate to the effect that one of the students in the junior classes had gone missing. The news reached me quite early, for the person in question happened to be in my dormitory.

Later, further details emerged. He had left the previous day to visit a friend at the Mfantsiman Girls' School. Unusually, he had failed to return. Since then all contact with him had been lost. The dormitory captain reported the matter to the housemaster.

Just before the housemaster could take further action, two police officers came to the school to find out whether anyone there was missing. They went on to explain that the authorities at the main hospital in the city had notified them about the unclaimed body of a young victim from a traffic accident that had occurred the previous evening.

Eventually the dead boy was identified as the missing student.

Still later, details emerged regarding the circumstances of his death. At the end of his visit, he had waited at a bus station to catch a bus to Cape Coast when a saloon car passed by and the driver offered him a lift. They had gone only a few kilometres when the vehicle was involved in a serious accident. Both occupants of the vehicle were killed instantly.

Before the body of our companion was driven to his home town for burial, a memorial service was held in the large school chapel in his honour. At one stage in the solemn service we were permitted to file past the body to pay our last respects to the dead boy.

Up to that time, I had witnessed only a couple of funeral ceremonies at Mpintimpi. As the dead boy lay in state, various mourners drew near to pay their respects. Children were generally not permitted to draw too close.

It was the second time I experienced a close confrontation with the dead – readers may recall the case of the young lad killed by the vehicle I was travelling on from Accra to Oda. Our classmate, who a couple of days before had been going about his life like any young person of his age, now lay motionless before us. All of a sudden the awareness that life could end very suddenly came home to me pretty powerfully and gave me food for thought.

Dissecting rabbits for valuable points

❖

Preparations for the GCE 'A'-Level examination intensified as from January 1978. I left nothing to chance; indeed, I left no stone unturned in my preparations. I was determined to pass well to ensure admission to one of the two medical schools in the country at that time.

Finally, towards the end of May, the GCE 'A'-Level examinations got under way.

Though several years have elapsed, I still remember that our main task in practical biology was to dissect a rabbit and name all its internal organs. I still remember how I initially put my rabbit to sleep with the help of chloroform and began, with the help of the instruments provided me, to open the bowels of the poor mammal.

I do not know what organisations such as the Society for the Prevention of Cruelty to Animals and the like would make of this revelation. Well, I was simply given a task to perform to get my grades. In the forefront of my thoughts was how to get the job done well so as to score the maximum points. All other thoughts were secondary.

Did I perform well in that assignment? I cannot give a definite answer to that since it formed only a part of the whole examination. Judging from the fact that it was only in Biology that I met my personal target not to achieve anything below grade B in the four subjects I offered, my guess is that I must have done well in the practical exam.

-56-
Bye-bye second-cycle club

❖

O n one sunny day in June 1978, with a mild breeze from the vast Atlantic ocean about two kilometres away from the gates of Mfantsipim blowing in my face to provide some relief from the scorching African heat, I packed, with the assistance of the driver, my *chop box* and *airtight*, the two companions that had accompanied me since my first journey to the boarding school, into the boot of the taxi I had flagged down moments before. Soon we were on our way to the 'Central Lorry Station' about a kilometre away.

On our arrival, I boarded a 33-seat Mercedes bus, which happened to be the first in a queue of a few other buses of the same make. After waiting for about half an hour, the last available seat was filled. Not long after that the driver got into his seat, turned the ignition key and got the motor running. Soon, he was driving the vehicle along the narrow streets of the coastal city.

Finally, I was putting behind me the era of my secondary school education. As I headed home, I looked forward to being admitted to medical school in October that year. I was confident I would do well enough in my 'A'-Levels to enable me to gain admission to either the well-established medical school in Accra or the newly opened medical faculty at the University in Kumasi. I saw in my mind's eye the realisation of my long-cherished dream, of becoming a doctor and using my profession to help improve the healthcare provision not only in the area I grew up in, but in the whole country.

Ordinary mortal that I am, not imbued with the ability to see into the future, how could I have the tiniest idea of what lay ahead of me?

It is true that I did indeed end up training to become a doctor; the path I had to tread to achieve that goal was, however, far different to the one that I ever imagined. Instead of the straightforward ride via either the University of Ghana medical school in Accra or the University of Science and Technology medical school in Kumasi, I had to tread a tortuous path that took me a little over six years!

Whoever is interested in a detailed account of my experience from the end of my Sixth Form education till my matriculation at medical school six years later is welcome to read my book *Medical School at Last.*

For those who may not find the time to do so, a brief overview of what happened follows.

I did not gain admission to medical school in Ghana as I had anticipated. Later on, I was offered a scholarship to study medicine in the Soviet Union, but unfortunately my name was deleted from the final list just when I was rejoicing over the new development in my life.

Acting on the advice of a friend who informed me I could study medicine in Germany without the need to pay tuition fees, I left Ghana for Nigeria to work with the aim of saving enough money to buy a plane ticket for Germany.

In the end I did indeed make it to Germany. There, after facing a catalogue of problems that culminated in my near deportation back to Ghana, I finally enrolled at the Hanover Medical School in October 1984.

EPILOGUE: insights of a grey-haired old-timer – freely received, freely imparted

❖

I f I have any advice for any young person who may be beginning his/ her academic journey, or who may already be in the middle of it, I will stress that there are no shortcuts to success. The saying, of course, is true not only in the area of academic endeavours but also for life in general.

It is an indisputable fact that some are more advantaged when it comes to academic prowess. There are indeed those endowed with photographic memories, those capable of remembering every detail, even the trivial details that they read or hear about – indeed, those of our race blessed with *record-breaking* IQs, those capable of doing their doctorates in their teens.

Such people are certainly the exceptional cases of our age. For the ordinary student like you and me, however, the fact remains that one can hardly avoid intensive preparation if one is to achieve academic success.

'Sew in tears and reap in joy' is an old adage.

Just as the farmer has to shed sweat to cultivate his land and spend time to sew before he/she can reap the harvest, so academic success, on the whole, comes only with hard work and dedication to our books.

Unless one believes it is possible to cheat in an exam, one cannot just sit back idly and hope that, one way or another, the knowledge required to pass that particular test will, somehow, be drawn to the brain without effort.

Spending hours on end to learn for my exams was by no means the most delightful experience I ever had! Indeed, on not a few occasions, when on the day prior to an important examination I had spent several hours of the day revising my notes only to realise towards the latter part of the day there was still a great deal of material that I still needed to go through before the dawn of the next day, I paused for a while to reflect on the whole concept of examinations as we have it now.

Why, I wonder, has our civilisation not come up with any other method of testing the individual's knowledge in their areas of study, than resorting to methods that may well be described as bordering on mental torture? So long as no alternative has been developed, however, one has no other choice but to play by the rules.

It is not an exercise in futility though. Apart from the joy of passing an examination, the qualification one obtains after the 'brain torture' will surely pave the way to many favours and privileges in later life.

A doctor working in a hospital is usually called upon by a nurse to sign a prescription. In most cases, the nurse may also be very aware of the workings of the medication concerned as well as the side effects – but he/she dare not sign it, if only for legal reasons! She would indeed be going beyond her competence. In such situations, I look back to the nights when I sat behind a pile of books revising for my medical examinations. The *mental torture* had, after all, not been in vain.

So, my young compatriot, if you are in similar circumstances and find yourself facing enormous pressure preparing for an impending examination, I urge you not to give up. Instead, you would do well to persevere to the end, for indeed your efforts will definitely not be in vain.